George Robert Stow Mead

The World-Mystery

Four Essays

George Robert Stow Mead

The World-Mystery
Four Essays

ISBN/EAN: 9783744731522

Printed in Europe, USA, Canada, Australia, Japan

Cover: Foto ©ninafisch / pixelio.de

More available books at **www.hansebooks.com**

THE
WORLD-MYSTERY

FOUR ESSAYS

BY

G. R. S. MEAD, B.A., M.R.A.S.

LONDON:
THEOSOPHICAL PUBLISHING SOCIETY,
7, DUKE STREET, ADELPHI, W.C.

MADRAS: "THEOSOPHIST" OFFICE, ADYAR.
BENARES: THE THEOSOPHICAL PUBLISHING SOCIETY.
1895

CONTENTS.

	PAGE
THE WORLD-SOUL	1
THE VESTURES OF THE SOUL	81
THE WEB OF DESTINY	113
TRUE SELF-RELIANCE	143

Ashcharyyavat pashyati kashchidenam
Âshcharyyavad vadati tathaiva chânyah
Âshcharyyavach chainamanyah shrinoti
Shrutvâpyenam veda na chaiva kashchit.

One sees this as a wonder,
As a wonder, too, one speaks of it,
As a wonder one hears of it,
And having heard, knows it not anyone.

BHAGAVAD GÎTÂ, II. 29.

Ὡς οὖν ἐγένετο . . πρὸς τὴν γῆν εἰπεῖν, ὥσπερ ἤκουσεν, ὅτι 'Πὰν ὁ μέγας τέθνηκεν'· οὐ φθῆναι δὲ παυσάμενον αὐτὸν, καὶ γενέσθαι μέγαν οὐχ ἑνὸς ἀλλὰ πολλῶν στεναγμὸν ἅμα θαυμασμῷ μεμιγμένον.

And so he called out to the land, as he had heard, "Pan, the Great, is dead." And hardly had he ceased, when there arose a mighty cry, not of one, but of many, mingled with wonderment.

PLUTARCH, ON THE CESSATION OF ORACLES, XVII.

Ἰδού, μυστήριον ὑμῖν λέγω.

Behold, I tell you a mystery.

I. CORINTHIANS, XV. 51.

THE WORLD-SOUL.

The task that I propose to myself is no light one; it is no less than to discuss some of the opinions of my fellow-men on Deity, and to point out, if possible, some common ground of agreement or reconciliation between the innumerable ideas put forward on this inexhaustible topic. I shall not write either as an avowed monotheist, pantheist, theist, or atheist, for I conceive that a real student of theosophy is sufficiently imbued with the spirit of the great law of expansion and progress, not to condemn himself or herself to the narrowing limits of any of these sectarian ideas, which cannot fail to bring him in conflict with the prejudices of some section or other of his brother-men.

I hope to find this common ground of agreement, for at any rate the theist, pantheist, or monotheist, in the concept of the World-Soul, *in one or other of its aspects;* although I despair of finding much sympathy from the so-called atheist, whose intellectual negation is frequently, if not invariably, stultified by his actions. For do we not find the avowed atheist searching for the reason of that which he denies to have any intelligent operation; do we not find him frequently striving for an ideal which can never be attained, if, as he supposes, the present is the outcome of the past interaction of blindly driving force and matter? Why, again, should he work for the improvement of the race if that race, as he himself, is to depart into the void together with the producer of his and its consciousness? For the body dies and the earth will also die. And if consciousness is a product of organized matter, then the disruption of that organism means inevitably the dissipation of consciousness. Why, then, this effort to benefit that which must, on his own hypothesis, tend inevitably to annihilation?

From the materialists, then, this essay, perchance, will gain little intellectual sympathy, although I may venture to hope that the ideals of their fellow-men, which will be brought forward, will meet, if not with reverential consideration, at least with respect. Nor will it be any part of my task to criticize, except in the briefest manner, any of the crude expressions of man's aspiration to the Divine, but rather to put forward a number of instances of the more perfect expressions of great minds and great teachers who have in some measure sensed the actuality of that mysterious bond that makes all men one.

First, then, let me say that the term World-Soul is not intended in this essay to carry the technical meaning of the platonic or neoplatonic All-Soul or Soul of the Universals (ψυχὴ τοῦ παντός or τῶν ὅλων); and so in order to express in some way what the term World-Soul is intended to mean, it will be necessary to give a meaning to the words "soul" and "world." By "soul" is intended the underlying "something" under every manifested form, that something which is the life, consciousness or intelligence, or whatever term is preferred, which makes it that form and no other. Nor should we exclude anything, not even that which in these latter days is called "inanimate," from our sympathy, for to our greater Selves naught that exists, nay, not even the grain of sand, is in-*animate*, for then it would be *soul*-less, and the Divine would have been excluded from part of itself.

And now let us start with ourselves in our enquiry, where we find a soul encased in a body, a body made of many "lives," of infinite infinitesimal cells, each the "form" of a soul. And yet the soul of man is not *composed* of these "lives"; the consciousness of man is not simply the product or sum of their consciousness, nor is his intelligence a compound of their intelligence. The soul of man is one, a self-centred unit, indestructible, imperishable, self-motive; it dies not nor comes into being.

Next, let us, taking this as a starting-point, use analogy to aid us, as we pass within, into the region of ideas. For analogy is the only method we can employ, if we wish to widen our understanding, and without it we might well doubt the possibility of knowledge. Every thing, or rather every soul, is the mirror of every other soul, just as in the Monadology of Leibnitz; and if it were not that a knowledge of one soul comprises the knowledge of all other souls, and that kosmos is contained potentially in every atom, then were our striving towards wisdom vain and our aspiration to reality likewise vain. Taking, then, the example of the human soul, enshrined in a universe of "lives," whether we regard it as it were a sun in the midst of its system, or as an ocean of light in which the "lives" are bathed, let us try to conceive that there is another and more mighty Life, a Divine Soul, of which the human souls are "lives," and which we may term the Soul of Humanity. And yet this Soul is not made up of the souls of men, but is a unit of itself, self-motive, and itself and naught else. Further—for the human mind is so constituted that nothing short of infinitude can suffice it—that this Divine Soul is in its turn a Life, one of an infinite number of "Lives" of a like degree, that enshrine a SOUL transcending them as much as man transcends the "lives" of the universe of his body. And further still, that that which transcends the Divine is, in its turn, . . . But why go further? Is not the series infinite? Where can we set the term, or place a boundary, or limit infinitude? "So far shalt thou go!" and then the mind loses itself in the stupendous height of its soaring and must return to earth to rest its wings.

Thus towards infinity we rise in our ideation,

conceiving every atom as the shrine of a soul; every stone, animal, man; every globe, and system, and universe; every system of universes, and universe of systems—as the shrine of a Soul. For our universe is neither the first nor the last of its kind; their number is infinite. And when the consummation of our present universe is perfected there will be "another Word on the tongue of the Ineffable," for the Ineffable speaks infinitely, or, as our Brâhman brethren say, there are "crores of crores of Brahmâs," or universes.

Thus an infinity in one direction of thought, and equally so an infinity in the other direction. For are not the "lives" of the body, too, the souls of a universe of other invisible "lives"; and these, each in its turn, the suns of still more invisible universes, until the infinitely small blends with the infinitely great and all is One.

Perhaps you may have thought that in this concept we have nothing but an infinite series of eternally separated entities; of infinite division; of a chaos of multiplicity; of a stupendous separateness? This might be so if it stood alone; but as in all things here below, we can have no manifestation without the help of contraries, we must take its twin concept to complete it.

In pluribus Unum et Unum in pluribus; One in many and in many One. "The *essential unity of all souls with the Over-Soul*" is a fundamental postulate of the Wisdom of all ages. That is to say all souls are one in essence, whatever forms they may ensoul. But what is more; what is almost an overpowering thought, necessary though it be to universal progress; not only the human soul, but even the soul of the very grain of dust has the potentiality of expanding its consciousness into the All-consciousness. Every soul is endowed with the power of giving and receiving with respect to every other soul; of passing through every stage of consciousness; of *expanding;* just as the One, the All-Soul, so to say, *contracted* itself into manifestation, into the Many, subordinating itself to itself, that every soul might know and become every other soul, by virtue of that Love which is the cause of existence.

Thus, then, every soul aspires to union with its own essence; and this constitutes the religious spirit of mankind; and also our love of wisdom and our search for certainty. This constitutes that Path to the Knowledge of Divine Things, which we to-day call Theosophy; that synthesis of true religion, philosophy and science; of right aspiration, right thought and right observation, which the world is ever blindly seeking.

The World-Soul, then, for us, is the One Soul of Humanity, which will differ for each soul in proportion to the state of consciousness it has arrived at. No two souls are alike, just as no two blades of grass or grains of sand are alike, for then, as has been well said, there would be no reason why one should be in a particular place or state and not the other, and so the Reason of the universe be stultified.

The term "world," in our present enquiry, therefore, will be limited to the cycle of manifestation of our particular humanity, for this is our present world; the collective embodiment of that Divine Soul, which may consequently be referred to as the World-Soul.

This source of his being, this essence of his nature, this something that transcends himself in his highest self-consciousness, man calls by many names, of which the one which obtains most generally in the Western world, and in the English tongue, is "God."

And here, much as I shrink from hurting the feelings of any devout believer, I would protest against the tendency of nearly all unreflecting religionists to limit the illimitable, to crystallize the fountain of their being, and to materialize That, which it is blasphemy to name, much less to attempt to dress in the tawdry rags of our own mental equipment. There are those who will talk to you of "God" as they would of a personal acquaintance, who profess a familiarity that would outrage our feelings of decency if the object of their remarks were even a wise and holy man whom we had learned to reverence. There are others who have such limited notions of the Divine that they cling with desperation to terms that have their origin in the vulgarest misunderstanding, and who dub those who will not use their Shibboleths as "atheists," simply because they cannot understand that there is a reverence of the mind that transcends terms of the emotions; that there is an aspiration that transcends all endeavour to give the names of human qualities to That which is beyond all qualities, and to which their pious jargon is blasphemy. If such reverence is "atheism," then we had better change our terms and cease to use words that no longer possess meaning.

Let all men agree that no definition is possible, and that any enunciation of the mystery is but a temporary stepping stone to higher and still higher things, and there will no longer be seen the sad spectacle of human beings trying to pour the ocean into a waterpot.

For after all what do men fear in the desperation with which they cling to such limiting terms? To me they appear to fear that, where all is so vague and abstract, the goal they propose to themselves would, without definition, seem too far off for them to ever hope to reach it. But surely they have the infinitude within their own nature? Is there not a "Christ" potential in every man which is his true Self; and beyond, the "Fatherhood"; and beyond, the "Father of all Fatherhoods"; and beyond— Infinitude? But all within the nature and in the essence of every man; nothing is without, nothing which is not of the same essence; all is That . . . ! Is it so strange to "go home"?

Is it an abstract void, a negation, to know

the Self's true Being? Or, on the other hand, is this a mere exaggeration of the personal man? Is this dictated by self-pride and self-conceit? If such reverent aspiration is thus condemned by any, they will first have to show that the great world-teachers have lied, for the word of no lesser men can come before their teaching. One and all, the great teachers have inculcated this wisdom; and it requires but little study to find how admirably it explains all the apparent contradictions in the exoteric expressions of the world-scriptures.

"Be humble if thou wouldst attain to wisdom." Yes, but do not debase yourself; humility is not slavishness; reverence is not fawning. How can Deity take pleasure in that which a noble-minded man could never view without the greatest pity? "I am but as a worm in thy sight," David is made to say, and there are those who rejoice to echo the words, and declare that without the "Grace of God," they must continue worms.

But how can even the body, much less the *man*, the mind, or thinker, be so debased? Each is most honourable in its own dominion, and only dishonourable in proportion as it fails to "do its mystery" in sacrifice to the Self, whose "Grace" is its very life and being and the well-spring of its action. It is the duty of man to "worship" the Deity and not to grovel. To present that which is "worthy" to the Self, and not to delight in debasement

"And so . . . with fear and trembling work out your own salvation: for the worker in you, both as to willing and working for well-pleasing, is Deity."

(ὥστε. . . μετὰ φόβου καὶ τρόμου τὴν ἑαυτῶν σωτηρίαν κατεργάζεσθε. Θεός γάρ ἐστιν ὁ ἐνεργῶν ἐν ὑμῖν καὶ τὸ θέλειν καὶ τὸ ἐνεργεῖν ὑπὲρ τῆς εὐδοκίας.—*Philippians* ii. 12, 13.)

And if that worker is the Divine Self, what reason is there that it should humble itself, or debase itself, for the very power that makes man work out his own salvation is that Deity itself?

We shall now be able to understand the words of Krishna, in the *Bhagavad Gîtâ* (vii. 21, 22):

"Whichever form of deity a worshipper longs with faith to worship, in that form I make his faith steady. Endowed with that faith he seeks to propitiate it in that form,

THE WORLD-SOUL. 13

and obtains therefrom his profitable desires which are in truth bestowed by me."

(Yo yo yám yám tanumbhaktah shraddhayárchchitum ichchhati,
Tasyá tasyáchalám shraddhám támeva viddhámyaham,
Sa tayá shraddhyá yuktustasyárádhanamíhate,
Labhate cha tatah kámán mayaiva vihitán hitán.)

And again (ix. 23) :

"Even those devotees of other deities who worship with faith, they too, O Son of Kunti, worship me indeed, though not as it is laid down."

(Yo'py anyadevatá bhaktá yajante shraddhyánvitáh,
Te'pi mámeva Kaunteya yajantyavidhipúrvakam.)

For Krishna is the World-Soul, the Self of all men (x. 20) :

"O Lord of doubt, I am the Self seated in the heart of all beings. I am the beginning and middle and end of all creatures."

(Aham átmá, Gudákesha, sarvabhútáshyasthitah,
Aham ádishcha madhyancha bhutánámanta eva cha.)

And now that no one may think that all this is a bald assertion and an unsupported statement, let us collect the evidences of wisdom from all climes and races and times, evidences as grand and unimpeachable as any that the modern scientist possesses for his five-sense facts.

The wealth of material is so great that it is difficult to cull a passage here and there and leave so much unnoticed. Neither is it easy to know in what order to take the world-religions; which to take first or which last.

As, however, we must start somewhere, let us begin with the oldest scriptures of our Âryan race, the Vedas, and then the oldest of the Purânas. Next let us take a glance at Taoism, the most mystical of the creeds of the far East; then pass to the Avesta, that ancient scripture of the Pârsis; and so on to Egypt; first quoting from the Zohar and other kabalistic writings which contain the wisdom of the Chaldæans and a key to the misunderstood scriptures of the Jews. Egypt will lead us to speak of the wisdom of Hermes and the Gnôsis of those who are now known generally as Gnostics; and this will lead to a quotation from Paul and some reference to the Greek and Roman philosophy, and the ancient systems of Orpheus and other

THE WORLD-SOUL.

great teachers. Finally we shall find identical ideas among the Scandinavian peoples, and a striking confirmation in Mohammedan Sufiism. All, all without exception, sensed the World-Soul, hymned of it, sought union therewith; for of what else could they speak? Only they glorified that which it was in its essence, and did not worship its grossest and most impermanent manifestation, the surface of five-sense nature. Such an idolatry was reserved to the latter end of the nineteenth century, when human intellect worships the ground its body treads on, the gross body of the World-Soul, and has forgotten whence it came and whither it will return. Our times are an age of the deification of matter and the consequent fall of ideals!

Thus, then, let us first turn to that mysterious link with the past, the *Rig Veda*. Who knows whence it came? Who can tell its origin? Perchance those who have kept the record since the great Deluge of Atlantis could name its transmitters, and tell of those who withdrew to the "Sacred Island."

Among prayers to the Supreme Principle, the World-Soul, first must come the famous Gâyatrî, "the holiest verse in the Vedas." It runs as follows, in what Wilson calls, " Sir William Jones's translation of a paraphrastic interpretation."

" Let us adore the supremacy of that Divine Sun, the Godhead, Who illuminates all, Who recreates all, from Whom all proceed, to Whom all must return, Whom we invoke to direct our understandings aright in our progress toward His holy seat." (Sir W. Jones' *Works*, xiii. 367.)

This mantra is found in the 10th Hymn of the 4th Ashtaka (Eighth) of the Samhitá (Collection) of the *Rig Veda*, not as in the above expanded paraphrase, but in an abbreviated form, for "such is the fear entertained of profaning this text, that copyists of the Vedas not unfrequently refrain from transcribing it," says Wilson. (*Vishnu Puràna*, ii. 251.) "It is the duty of every Bráhman to repeat it *mentally* in his morning and evening devotions," and it is to be suspected that the western world has not yet received the correct text, though Sir William Jones may have got a version nearer the truth than his successors. It is well known that the Bráhmans are the proudest and most

THE WORLD-SOUL.

exclusive people in the world where the secrets of their religion are concerned, and it is reasonable to suppose that a mantra that pertains to their initiation would not be lightly revealed.

The subtle metaphysical and mystical interpretations of this most sacred formula, especially those of the Vedânta School, testify to its sanctity. The number of interpretations also that the words of the mantra lend themselves to are almost innumerable. The phrasing, for instance, can be taken as neuter or masculine and so on.

Perhaps the spirit of the central thought of the oriental religious world may be further explained by another Hymn, translated by Sir William Jones. It reiterates that most stupendous intuition of the human mind, that feeling of identity with the World-Soul, in a magnificent litany which runs as follows :

"May that Soul of mine, which mounts aloft in my waking hours, as an ethereal spark, and which, even in my slumber, has a like ascent, soaring to a great distance, as an emanation from the light of lights, be united by devout meditation with the Spirit supremely blest, and supremely intelligent !

"May that Soul of mine, by an agent similar to which the low-born perform their menial works, and the wise, deeply versed in sciences, duly solemnize their sacrificial rite; that Soul, which was itself the primal oblation placed within all creatures, be united by devout meditation with the Spirit supremely blest, and supremely intelligent!

"May that Soul of mine, which is a ray of perfect wisdom, pure intellect and permanent existence, which is the unextinguishable light fixed within created bodies, without which no good act is performed, be united by devout meditation with the Spirit supremely blest, and supremely intelligent!

"May that Soul of mine, in which, as an immortal essence, may be comprised whatever has past, is present, or will be hereafter; by which the sacrifice, where seven ministers officiate, is properly solemnized, be united by devout meditation with the Spirit supremely blest, and supremely intelligent!

"May that Soul of mine, into which are inserted, like the spokes of a wheel in the axle of a car, the holy texts of the Vedas; into which is interwoven all that belongs to created forms,

THE WORLD-SOUL.

be united by devout meditation with the Spirit supremely blest, and supremely intelligent!

"May that Soul of mine, which, *distributed in other bodies*, guides mankind, as a skilful charioteer guides his rapid horses with reins; that Soul which is fixed in my breast, exempt from old age, and extremely swift in its course, be united, by divine meditation, with the Spirit supremely blest, and supremely intelligent!" (Sir W. Jones' *Works*, xiii. 372, 373.)

Such is an instance of the advanced theosophy of the Vedas, in the face of which it is difficult to understand the crude criticisms of the Weber-Müllerite School of materialistic scholarship, who would set it all down to the imaginings of a primitive pastoral people. The theosophical student is glad to turn to such a fair estimate as that of Barth, who says:

"Neither in the language nor in the thought of the *Rig Veda* have I been able to discover that quality of primitive natural simplicity which so many are fain to see in it. The poetry it contains appears to me, on the contrary, to be of a singularly refined character and artificially elaborated, full of allusions and reticences, of pretensions to mysticism and theosophic insight; and the manner of its expression is such as reminds one more frequently of the phraseology in use among certain small groups of initiated than the poetic language of a large community." (*The Religions of India*, p. xiii.)

Truly so; and perhaps before long the methods of the Veda may be better understood, and it will be recognized how that the powers of nature and the moral attributes of man are fitter symbols of a divine theogony than personifications which include all the vices and pettiness of animal-man.

As H. W. Wallis says (*Cosmogony of the Rig Veda*, p. 8):

"The deities of the *Rig Veda* differ essentially from the Gods of Greek or Scandinavian mythology and of the *Mahábhárata*, in the abstract and almost impersonal nature of their characters. They are little more than factors in the physical and moral order of the world, apart from which none, except perhaps Indra, has a self-interested existence."

To the Greek, Scandinavian and Mahábháratan deities, we may add the Pantheons of other nations as well, and also their Indras, Zeuses,

Jehovahs, and the rest, whose "self-interest" is explicable seeing that they were but the representations of the time-period or manifestations of a certain world, for there are crores of Brahmâs, Jupiters and Jehovahs in the ideal Kosmos. It is time that the western nations should remember their birth-place. We are not Semites but Âryans, a younger branch of the great Âryan Race, perchance, but still Âryans and not Semites. And being so we should remember the wisdom of our fathers and put aside the crude conceptions of the Semites as to Deity. Jehovah is in his place as the God of a small warlike nomad tribe, but entirely out of place in the Religion of those who profess to be followers of the Christ. It is high time to lay aside such gross anthropomorphism, which the learned Jews themselves rejected, as their Kabalah and Philo well testify. The curse of Christendom to-day is belief in this "jealous" and "self-interested" Jehovah as the One God, an idea alien to Âryan thought. Direful indeed has been the effect of the "curse" of the "chosen people" on their spoliators. They were robbed of their Scriptures, deprived of them by force, and the ravished maiden of the Semites, forced against her will into the arms of the marauding Âryans, has used her "magic arts" against the tribe that holds her prisoner, for to-day she imprisons the *minds* of those who hold her *body* captive.

In other words, the western nations, being the youngest of the Âryan family, and lusty only in body, have in their ignorance worshipped the dead letter of that which they have not understood, and so debased their minds and characters with a bibliolatry scarce paralleled in the history of the world. Let us hope that this is passed and that the end of the nineteenth century may see the "prodigal son" return "home," and chastened by the experience of his exile, show his real heredity in an activity that his more sluggish elder brother in the East, who has never left home, can never manifest in such abundance, because of his very passivity. The Âryans have an ancestral religion, and every Âryan in the West should see to it that he does not pursue after other Gods.

Of course I speak of the crude exoteric God of the Hebrew populus, and not of the Mystery Deity, the Father, preached to the Jews by the

Initiate, whom the West calls Jesus of Nazareth. For did he not say that his hearers were " of their father the Devil," for they were " Abraham's seed " and " Abraham " was the ruler of this world? Nor do I mean any disrespect to the Jews of to-day, who are no more the Jews of the Bible, than we are Goths or Vandals, or woad-besmeared Britons. I do not write about, or for, " bodies," I am writing for " minds " and " souls " whose ancestry is divine, and not of the Lord of the Body, call him by what name you will.

How long will the perverse mind of man persist in telling us the fashion in which " God created " the world; how long will men blasphemously speak of That which is unutterable, and degrade the majesty of their Divine Souls into the poor imaginings of the animal minds which think in terms of their gross bodies, and of naught else? More reverently indeed did our ancestors phrase the mystery when they were yet uncontaminated by the mire of their earthly tabernacles, and a huckstering commercialism and a pseudo-science that gropes, on hands and knees, with eyes fixed on the surface of things, had not dragged the ideals of humanity down to the dust. How different are the beginnings of cosmogony as sung of in the *Rig Veda!* The passage is familiar to western students in the noble verse of Colebrooke. The following, however, is another version :

"The non-existent was not, and the existent was not at that time; there was no air or sky beyond; what was covering in? and where? under shelter of what? was there water—a deep depth?

"Death was not nor immortality then, there was no discrimination of night and day: that one thing breathed without a wind of its own self; apart from it there was nothing else at all beyond.

"Darkness there was, hidden in darkness, in the beginning, everything here was an indiscriminate chaos; it was void covered with emptiness, all that was; that one thing was born by the power of warmth.

"So in the beginning arose desire, which was the first seed of mind; the wise found out by thought, searching in the heart, the parentage of the existent in the non-existent.

"Their line was stretched across; what was

THE WORLD-SOUL.

above? what was below? there were generators, there were mighty powers; *svadha*, [nature perhaps] below, the presentation of offerings above.

"Who knoweth it forsooth? who can announce it here? whence it was born, whence this creation is? The gods came by the creating of it (*i.e.*, the one thing); who then knoweth whence it is come into being?

"Whence this creation [lit. emission] is come into being, whether it was ordained or no—He whose eye is over all in the highest heaven, He indeed knoweth it, or may be He knoweth it not." (Wallis, *Cosmogony of the Rig Veda*, pp. 59, 60. [R. V., x. 129].)

Even such wooden translation cannot prevent the grandeur of the original occasionally peeping through, how much more noble then would be the translation of one who was whole-hearted in his version?

Notice the last lines. The World-Soul may know, or perchance even it knoweth not. For there are other World-Souls, and as among men most are ignorant of their own genesis so amid the World-Souls, some—the few perchance—may know, the many be ignorant; none knoweth absolutely but the One.

Passing next to a later Âryan Scripture, let us read how the great sect of the Vaishnavas hymn the deity, as written in the *Vishnu Purána* (I. i.):

"OM! glory to Him who dwells in all beings (Vâsudeva). Victory be to Thee, Thou heart-pervading one (Pundarîkâksha); adoration be to Thee, Thou cause of the existence of all things (Vishvabhâvana); glory be to Thee, Lord of the senses (Hrishîkesha), the Supreme Spirit (Mahâpurusha), the ancient of birth (Pûrvaja)."

And later in the same work we read (v. 14-16, Wilson's Translation):

"Salutation to Thee, Who art uniform and manifold, all-pervading, Supreme Spirit, of inconceivable glory, and Who art simple existence! Salutation to Thee, O inscrutable, Who art Truth, and the essence of oblations! Salutation to Thee, O Lord, Whose nature is unknown, Who art beyond Primeval Matter, Who existest in five forms,[1] as one with the

[1] These are given by Wilson (i. 3) as: 1. Bhûtâtman, one with created things, or Pundarîkâksha; 2. Pradhânâtman, one with Crude Nature, or Vishvabhâvana; 3. Indriyâtman, one with the Senses, Hrishîkesha; 4. Paramâtman, Supreme Spirit, or Mahâpurusha; and 5. Âtman, Living Soul, animating Nature, and existing before it, or Pûrvaja.

THE WORLD-SOUL.

Elements, with the Faculties, with Matter, with the Living Soul, with Supreme Spirit! Show favour, O Soul of the Universe, essence of all things, perishable or eternal, whether addressed by the designation of Brahmâ, Vishnu, Shiva, or the like. I adore Thee, O God Parameshvara, Supreme Lord, rather], Whose nature is indescribable, Whose purposes are inscrutable, Whose name, even, is unknown; for the attributes of appellation or kind are not applicable to Thee, Who art THAT, the supreme Brahma [neuter] eternal, unchangeable, uncreated [Aja, unborn, rather.] But as the accomplishment of our objects cannot be attained except through some specific form, Thou art termed by us Krishna, Achyuta [the Imperishable], Ananta [the Endless,] or Vishnu. Thou, unborn (divinity), art all the object of these impersonations; Thou art the Gods, and all other beings; Thou art the whole World; Thou art all. Soul of the Universe, thou art exempt from change; and there is nothing except Thee in this whole existence. Thou art Brahmâ [male], Pashupati [Shiva, 'Lord of (sacred) animals'], Aryaman, Dhâtri, and

28   THE WORLD-MYSTERY.

Vidhâtri;[1] thou art Indra,[2] Air, **Fire, the Regent of the Waters**;[3] the God of Wealth,[4] and Judge of the Dead;[5] and Thou, although but one,

---

[1] Aryaman and Dhâtri are two of the Twelve Âdityas, or Sons of Aditi, the " Mother," which were seven originally, Mârttânda, the "rejected" Sun being the eighth. Later they became the Twelve Sun Gods. Vidhâtri is the arranger or disposer, the Kosmokratôr or Demiurge, and is added as a title to Brahmâ, Vishvakarman and Kâma, the Erôs of the Orphic fragments. As Dr. Muir says: "This Kâma or Desire, not of sexual enjoyment, but of good in general, is celebrated in a curious hymn of the *Atharva Veda*: 'Kâma was born first [the Orphic Prôtogenes]. Him, neither gods, nor fathers, nor men have equalled. Thou art superior to these, and for ever great.'"

[2] The "Zeus dwelling in the Æther" of Homer (Ζεὺς αἰθέρι ναίων—*Iliad*, ii. 412), in the Æther, the abode of the Gods. The Pater Æther of Virgil.

[3] Varuna (Ooaroona), the Regent of the Astral Waters of Space, the Uranus (Ouranos) of the Greeks, who was emasculated and dethroned by Cronus (Time) at the instigation of his mother and wife Gæa (Earth). From the drops of his blood sprang the Gigantes or Titans, the early Races, and from the foam that gathered round his limbs in the sea, sprang Venus-Aphrodite (Hesiod, *Theog.*, 180-195.)

[4] Kuvera, the keeper of the treasures of the Earth, lord of the Earth, called the Egg of Jewels, Ratnagarbha.

[5] Antaka the "Ender," a title of Yama, the "Restrainer," the Judge of the Dead. A Vedic Hymn tells us that Yama "was the first of men that died, and the first that departed to the (celestial) world." As Dowson says: "He it was who found out the way to the home which cannot be taken away. Those who are now born (follow) by their own paths to the place whither our ancient fathers have departed." This, in the more direct tradition of the Vedas, is a glyph of the Third Race that brought

". . . . . death into the world
 And all our woe, with loss of Eden

presidest over the world, with various energies addressed to various purposes. Thou, identical with the solar ray, createst the universe; all elementary substance is composed of Thy qualities; and Thy supreme form is denoted by the imperishable term Sat. . . . To Him who is one with True Knowledge; who is, and is not, perceptible (sat and asat, 'real' and 'unreal'), I bow. Glory be to Him, the Lord Vâsudeva!"

The same strain of adoration is still further emphasized in the hymn of the Yogins when Vishnu, in the Boar Incarnation, or Varâha Avatâra, raised the Earth out of the Waters (*Ibid.*, i. 63):

"THOU ART, O God, there is no supreme condition but Thou."

Or again, as the God Brahmâ prays to the Supreme Hari (Vishnu) (*Ibid.*, i. 139):

"We glorify Him, Who is all things; the

But Yama, in the later traditions Pitripati and Pretarâja, the "Lord of the Manes" and "King of the Ghosts," was also Dharmarâja, "King of Justice," our *Selves* who judge ourselves, in the clear Akâshic Light, while Chitragupta (the "Hidden Painting or Writing"), the Scribe of Yama, reads the imprint of our virtues and our vices from the Agrasandhâni or "Great Record," the Tablets of the Imperishable Memory of the Astral Light. Yama is represented as of a green colour, clothed with red.

Lord supreme over all; unborn, imperishable; the protector of the mighty ones of creation, the unperceived,[1] indivisible Nârâyana; the smallest of the small, the largest of the largest Elements; in Whom are all things; from Whom are all things; Who was before existence; the God Who is all beings; Who is the end of ultimate objects; Who is beyond final Spirit, and is one with Supreme Soul; Who is contemplated, as the cause of final liberation, by sages anxious to be free."

As the Avatâra Krishna, He is hymned of by Indra after his defeat by Him. *(Ibid.,* v. 103.)

"Who is able to overcome the unborn, unconstituted Lord, Who has willed to become a mortal, for the good of the world?"

And when Krishna is *nailed* by the arrow to the *tree*, and the Kali Yuga begins, this is how Arjuna, his beloved companion, laments the departure of the Christ-Spirit, of That which "unites Entity to Non-entity." (*Ibid.,* v. 161, 162.)

"Hari, Who was our strength, our might,

---

[1] Aprakâsha: Fitzedward Hall tells us that the commentator explains this to mean "self-illuminated."

our heroism, our prowess, our prosperity, our brightness, has left us, and departed. Deprived of him, our friend, illustrious, and ever kindly speaking, we have become as feeble as if made of straw. Purushottama, who was the living vigour of my weapons, my arrows, and my bow, is gone. As long as we looked upon Him, fortune, fame, wealth, dignity never abandoned us. But Govinda is gone from among us. . . . Not I alone, but Earth, has grown old, miserable and lustreless, in His absence. Krishna . . . . is gone!"

Let us next pass to China and the Far East. Lao-tze, perhaps the greatest of the Chinese masters, teaches as follows, in his sublime work the *Tao-teh-king*, or "The Book of the Perfection of Nature" (*A Study on the Popular Religion of the Chinese*, by J. J. M. de Groot: translated from the Dutch in *Les Annales du Musée Guimet*, ii. 692 *et seq.*):

"There was a time when Heaven and Earth did not exist, but only an unlimited Space in which reigned absolute immobility. All the visible things and all that which possess existence, were born in that Space from a powerful principle, which existed by Itself, and from Itself developed Itself, and which made the heavens revolve and preserved the universal life; a principle as to which philosophy declares we know not the name, and which for that reason it designates by the simple appellation Tao, which we may nearly describe as the Universal Soul of Nature, the Universal Energy of Nature, or simply as Nature."

And in speaking of the mysterious Tao, the That which cannot be translated, the nameless principle, we may with advantage quote from an essay by a sympathetic scholar, who writes as follows (*Taoism*, an essay by Frederic H. Balfour, in *Religious Systems of the World*, p. 77):

"We are told that it has existed from all eternity. Chuang-tze, the ablest writer of the Taoist school, says that there never was a time when it was not. Lao-tze, the reputed founder of Taoism, affirms that the image of it existed before God Himself. It is all pervasive; there is no place where it is not found. It fills the Universe with its grandeur and sublimity; yet it is so subtle that it exists in all its plenitude in the tip of a thread of gossamer. It causes the sun and moon to revolve in their appointed orbits, and gives life to the most microscopic

THE WORLD-SOUL. 33

insect. Formless, it is the source of every form we see; inaudible, it is the source of every sound we hear; invisible, it is that which lies behind every external object in the world; inactive, it yet produces, sustains and vivifies every phenomenon which exists in all the spheres of being. It is impartial, impersonal, and passionless; working out its ends with the remorselessness of Fate, yet abounding in beneficence to all."

And later on he quotes as follows from Chuang-tze:

"There was a time when all things had a beginning. The time when there was yet no beginning had a beginning itself. There was a beginning to the time when the time that had no beginning had not begun. There is existence and there is also non-existence. In the time which had no beginning there existed Nothing. . . . When the time which had no beginning had not yet begun, then there also existed Nothing. Suddenly, there was Nothing; but it cannot be known, respecting existence and non-existence, what was certainly existing and what was not."

I have given the above as a specimen of

subtle metaphysical speculation, and also as an example to show the utter inadequacy of words to express ideas. The mind loses itself in endeavouring to transcend itself, even to the extent of appearing entirely incomprehensible to those who have not seriously approached the contemplation of that supreme intuition of humanity, the essential Unity of all things.

But no one should think that this No-thing is an empty abstraction and mere negation; it transcends our finite concepts, but is no less the One Reality because of that. It is the right perception of these great problems that inspires such noble concepts of existence and calm contemplation of "death" as those expressed in the words of Lieh-tze:

"Death is to life as going away is to coming. How can we know that to die here is not to be born elsewhere? How can we tell whether, in their eager rush for life, men are not under a delusion? How can I tell whether, if I die to-day, my lot may not prove far preferable to what I was when I was originally born? . . . . Ah! men know the dreadfulness of death; but they do not know its rest. . . . How excellent is it, that from all antiquity Death has

THE WORLD-SOUL.

been the common lot of men! It is repose for the good man, and a hiding-away of the bad. Death is just a going home again. The dead are those who have gone home, while we, who are living, are still wanderers." (*Op. cit.*, p. 81.)

Aye; death is indeed a "going home," but a "going home" that need not be delayed until the body dies. Some theosophists have heard of those who "go home" when they have "died" to their lower natures; and then they know the real nature of this illusory existence, although, as the Rishi Nârada reported, it was very pleasant for those "who had forgotten their birth-place." The Soul of Humanity, the World-Soul, weeps for her children, who forget their Mother and, "prodigal sons" that they are, fill their bellies with husks of the swine.

Continuing our depredations from the shelves of the world-library, we pass to ancient Persia or whatever country gave to the world the wisdom of the old Avesta. Written in a language hardly yet plainly decipherable, it may well be approached to the Vedas in antiquity, and its language be referred to one of the first branchlets of the mother of Sanskrit.

In the Avesta of the Pârsis, Zarvâna Akarna,

"Time without Bounds," is the ineffable All; in this arises Ahura Mazda, the World-Soul, whose names are many. He is The Being and the One Existence; the One, Who was, Who is and Who shall always be. He is Pure Spirit and the Spirit of Spirits; Omniscient and Omnipotent, the Supreme Sovereign. He is beneficent, benevolent, and merciful to all. In the *Dinkard* (ii. 81), He is described as:

"Supreme sovereign, wise creator, supporter, protector, giver of good things, virtuous in actions and merciful."

Let us now see what the Kabalah has to teach us, and mark the difference of its great large spirit from the glorification of the "jealous God," the "God of armies," to whom so-called Christian nations pray to bless their respective arms in fratricidal wars. To-day sees Christian Europe armed to the teeth in honour of Jehovah, while the "Father" of Jesus, the "God of Love" is set on one side and forgotten.

Solomon ben Yehudah Ibn Gebirol, of Cordova, the greatest of the mediæval kabalistic adepts, thus sings of the World-Soul, or the Supreme Principle, in one of his philosophical

THE WORLD-SOUL.

Hymns, called "The Kether Malkuth," or "Crown of the Kingdom."

"Thou art God, Who supports, by Thy Divinity, all the things formed, and sustains all the existences by Thy Unity. Thou art God, and there is not any distinction established between Thy Divinity, Thy Unity, Thy Eternity, and Thy Existence; because all is only one mystery, and, although the names may be distinct, all have only one meaning. Thou art Wise, Wisdom which is the fountain of life, floweth from Thee, and compared with Thy Wisdom, all the knowledge of mankind is foolishness. Thou art Wise, being from all eternity, and Wisdom was always nourished by Thee. Thou art Wise, and Thou hast not acquired Thy Wisdom from another than Thyself. Thou art Wise, and from Thy Wisdom Thou hast made a determining Will, as the workman or artist does, to draw the Existence from the No-Thing, as the light which goes out of the eye extends itself. Thou didst draw from the Source of Light without the impression of any seal, that is, form, and Thou madest all without any instrument." (Myer's *Qabbalah*, p. 3.)

See how differently the mind of this learned

Jew regarded the "creation" of the Universe from the absurdity of the dead-letter dogma of "creation out of nothing." Just as the artist fashions the pot out of the clay, so does the Deity, out of its Wisdom which is Itself, emanate or evolve a determining Will to draw the "Existence" from the "No-Thing," the potentiality of that same Wisdom, for it is No-Thing in that it transcends all and every *thing* we can think of, that is to say, the highest conceptions of human thought. But It is no more "Nothing" than is Deity the "Unconscious." The No-Thing is not "nothing," the Non-conscious is not "unconscious," but both are attributes expressive of our ignorance, while asserting that That transcends all things and all consciousness.

So that we should do well to bear in mind the wise words of the *Zohar* and apply the injunction contained therein to the words of the Hymn of the master of the Kabalah we have just cited, being well assured that he would have permitted none of his pupils to take the words of his instruction for the real mystery itself. Says the *Zohar* (III. fol. 152*b*; in Myer's *Qabbalah*, p. 102):

"Woe to the man who sees in the Thorah (Law) only simple recitals and ordinary words. . . . Each word of the Thorah contains an elevated meaning and a sublime mystery. The recitals of the Thorah are the vestments of the Thorah. Woe to him who takes this garment for the Thorah itself."

Or, again, as Origen, perhaps the most philosophical of all the Church Fathers, writes:

"Where can we find a mind so foolish as to suppose that God acted like a common husbandman, and planted a paradise in (the Garden of) Eden, towards the East; and placed in it a Tree of Life visible and palpable, so that one tasting of the fruit by the bodily teeth obtained life? And, again, that one was a partaker of good and evil by masticating what was taken from the tree? And if God is said to walk in the paradise in the evening, and Adam to hide himself under a tree, I do not suppose that anyone doubts that these things figuratively indicate certain mysteries, the history having taken place in appearance, and not literally." (Origen's Works, Clark's Ed., cited, 315 *et seq.*, Bk. iv. c. 2.)

But then Origen was once the disciple of

Pantænus, after the latter's return from India, who was also the teacher of Clement.

Yet one more citation from the *Zohar*, before we leave the Kabalah, in order to vindicate the writers of that famous collection of books called the Bible, which is almost universally misunderstood.

"The Ancient of the Ancients, the Unknown of the Unknown, has a form, yet also has not any form. It has a form through which the Universe is maintained. It also has not any form as It cannot be comprehended." (*Zohar*, "Idra Zuta," iii. 288a; Myer, *ibid.*, p. 274.)

Passing from Chaldæa and Judæa to Egypt and its hoary wisdom, this is what M. Gaston Maspéro, the learned French Egyptologist, in his *Histoire d'Orient*, writes concerning the ideas of the Egyptians on the Soul of the World:

"In the beginning was the Noon, the Primordial Ocean, in the infinite depths of which floated the germs of all things. From all eternity God generated Himself and gave birth to Himself in the bosom of this liquid mass, as yet without form and without use. This God of the Egyptians, One Being only, perfect, endowed with knowledge and unfallacious intelligence, incomprehensible in so far as no one can say in what He is incomprehensible. He is the One Only One, He Who exists essentially, Who alone lives in substance, the sole generator in the Heaven and on the Earth Who is not generated, the Father of Fathers, the Mother of Mothers." (Quoted by M. E. Amélineau in his *Essai sur le Gnosticisme Egyptien*, in the series of *Les Annales du Musée Guimet*, Tom. xiv. 282.)

The Supreme God of the Mysteries whom the Greeks named Ammon, the Egyptians called Amen. As M. E. de Rougé says (*Mélanges d' Archéologie*, p. 72): "The name Amen means 'hidden,' 'enveloped,' and by extension 'mystery.' . . . . This God then was called Amen because He represented all that was most secret in Divinity." In a Hymn to Ammon Ra, speaking of the name Amen, it is said (Grébaut, *Hymne à Ammon Ra*): "Mysterious is his name even more than his births." And, in the invocations, which M. Naville has collected under the title of *Litanie du Soleil*, the same God is called "Lord of the hidden spheres," the "Mysterious One," the "Hidden." (Amélineau, *op. cit.*, p. 285.)

Here also must be appended a magnificent Hymn to the Sun, the symbol of the World-Soul, in which we can see peeping through the mysticism of both the initiatory Psalms of the Old Testament and certain concepts in the New. Thus it runs:

"The Princes of Heaven all daily behold the glory of the King's Crown, upon the head of Thee, the Mighty Prince, which is the Crown of Power, which is the Crown of the Endurance of Thy Government, an Image of Thy might.

"Songs of praise to the Creator of Egypt, and of the Shining Bark of the Lord (the Sun). Make those to fear, who hate Thee, make Thine enemies to blush, Lord and Prince of the very shining Star-house; Thou Who hast joined together Thy plantation, Thou Who seest the Murderer of Thy Child of Man, the Righteous. Let me go to Thee; unite me with Thee; let me look upon Thy Sunlight, King of the Universe!

"Praise to Thy Face, Beaming Light in the Firmament, to Thee, to the Shining Lord of the Heaven's Bark, to the Creator and Ruler

THE WORLD-SOUL.

Who renders justice to all men, who delight to see Thee walking in the Web of Thy Splendour." (From Uhlemann's *Book of the Dead*, as quoted in Dunlap's *Söd: The Mysteries of Adoni*, p. 187.)

Let us now turn to another Book of Wisdom, and hear what Hermes, the thrice greatest,[1] has to tell us of the mystery. In the treatise called *Pœmandres*, the World-Mind, Pœmandres, the "Mind of the Absolute" (ὁ τῆς αὐθεντίας νοῦς), mirrored in the Higher Ego of the Initiate, thus speaks to his lower consciousness:

"Say well, O Thou! speaking such things. I myself, the Mind, am present with the holy and good, and pure and merciful, with those living piously; and my presence becomes a help; and forthwith they are cognizant of all things, and lovingly propitiate the Father, and give thanks, praising and singing hymns to Him in ranks [in their orders, rather], from affection; and before delivering over the body to its own death, they detest the senses, knowing their operations; or rather I, The Mind, will not suffer the operations of the body which

---

[1] On the Rosetta stone he is called simply "Great, Great, Great"—μέγας, μέγας, μέγας.

happen, to be accomplished; for being doorkeeper, I will shut out the incomings of the evil and base operations, cutting off desires."[1]

Although it is impossible in the short space at my disposal to attempt an analysis of the various passages cited, still I would briefly suggest to students a few hints as to interpretation. The Father is here, as in cognate schools of philosophical mysticism, the Âtma-Buddhi in Kosmos and Man, and the hymns the "music of the spheres" of man's septenary nature, which sing in harmony only when man becomes one with the great Soul of Nature. The idea is well expressed by Dryden, who writes:

"From harmony, from heavenly harmony,
  This universal frame began;
  From harmony to harmony,
  Through all the compass of the notes it ran,
  The diapason closing full in man."

The teaching, however, as to the loathing[2] of

---

[1] From Chambers' translation (p. 12), which is as accurate and painstaking as may be, considering the translator's strong sectarian bias. The *Pœmandres*, however, has yet to be translated by a true theosophical student.

[2] Μυσάττεσθαι is a very strong word, meaning to abominate, detest, loathe; used of filth and foulness.

the senses is different to the wiser instruction of the Upanishads, where we learn that both longing and detestation are equally bonds of attachment, and that pure freedom can never be won by such means.

Mark well also the curious expression that the Mind is the "door-keeper," both the great Mind and the mind of man; the one keeping the doors or gates of the great planes of the septenary universe, the other guarding the portals of the seven "principles." And here we may do well to call to mind H. P. Blavatsky's words: "In that mansion called the human body the brain is the front door, and the only one which opens out into Space." (*Lucifer*, vii. 182.)

Let us—as the preceding sentences naturally lead up to it—pause here a moment to learn the path of the Soul up to the "Father," when death overtakes the body, and when the seven corruptible are put off for the incorruptible, according to the Hermetic Gnôsis.

"'You have well taught me,' I said, 'all things as I desired, O Mind! But tell me further about the ascent that is to be.'

"To these things Pœmandres said: 'First,

indeed, in the dissolution of the body material, it delivers up the body itself unto alteration, the form which thou hast becomes invisible, and delivers the character deprived of energy to the demon (daimôn), and the senses of the body return back to their respective sources, becoming portions, and again united together with the energies. And passion and desire depart to the irrational nature.

"'And thus the residue hastens upwards through the Harmony, and gives up to the first zone the energy of increase and that of decrease; and to the second the machination of the evils and the fraud deënergized; and to the third the concupiscent deception deënergized; and to the fourth the pride of domineering without means of satisfaction; and to the fifth the unholy boldness and the rashness of the audacity; and to the sixth the evil covetings after wealth, deënergized; and to the seventh zone insidious falsehood.

"'And, then, denuded from the operations [energizings] of the Harmony, it becomes energizing at the eighth nature, having its proper power, and along with the entities [essences] hymning The Father. Those

THE WORLD-SOUL.

being present at this his coming there, rejoice together, and being made like to those who are with Him, he hears also the Powers who are above the eighth nature in a certain sweet voice hymning The God. And then in order they mount upward to The Father, and they deliver themselves up to the Powers, and becoming Powers they become in God. This is the good end of those attaining knowledge, to be made Divine. For the rest, why delayest thou? Is it not that having accepted all things, thou mayest become guide to those who are worthy; so that the race of mankind through thee may be saved by God?'" (Chambers, pp. 13, 14.)

One might almost think that the treatise was written by the same hand that inscribed for us that wonderful relic of Egyptian Gnosticism called the *Pistis Sophia*. Who can tell whence was the original source of this hoary tradition of wisdom?

The passage loses much in translation for the general reader, and it is difficult to recognise that nearly every word is a precise technical term, just as are the terms in the opening chapters of the Gospel according to John.

It is easy to see that the first paragraph

refers to the dissolution of the lower four principles, whereas the second paragraph refers to the seven aspects of the lower mind, and the last to the mysteries of the Higher Ego, of the Primordial Emanations in the Plerôma, of the Hierarchies of the Sons of the Mind, and of the supreme realisation of the Nirvâna of Âtma-Buddhi.

What the idea of the Egyptian Initiate was concerning this attainment, and how difficult it is to treat of such lofty themes without the grossest self-contradictions, we may learn from the following passage :

" Holy The God, The Father of the Universals, Whose counsel is perfected by His own powers. Holy The God Who willeth to know and is known by His own. Holy Thou art Who by Word hast constituted the Entities. Thou art Holy, of Whom all nature was born as the image. Thou art Holy Whom the nature formed not. Thou art Holy Who art stronger than all power. Thou art Holy Who art greater than all excellence. Thou art Holy Who art superior to praises. Accept rational sacrifices pure from soul and heart, intent upon Thee, O unspeakable, ineffable, invoked by silence !" *(Ibid.,* pp. 15, 16.)

THE WORLD-SOUL.

The inability of human words to express that which must ever escape expression—for even the Universe itself is incapable of expressing It, seeing that there is an infinite number of Universes—and the failure of the human mind to express the Divine Mind are well shown in the following passage also:

"This the God is superior to a name; This the unmanifest; This the most manifest, to be contemplated by the mind; This visible to the eyes; This incorporeal, multicorporeal—yea, rather of every body; for there is nothing which This is not. For This is above all things. And because of this He has all names, that He is One Father, and because of this he has not a name that He is Father of all. Who, then, is able to bless, to sing praises of (εὐλογῆσαι) Thee, concerning Thee, or to Thee? Looking whither shall I bless Thee, above, below, within, without? for there is no condition, no place about Thee, nor anything else of the Entities; for all things are in Thee, all things from Thee, having given all things and receiving nothing; for Thou hast all things, and nothing that Thou hast not.

"When, O Father! shall I hymn Thee? for

neither Thine hour nor time is it possible to ascertain : concerning what also shall I hymn? concerning what things Thou hast made, or concerning those Thou hast not made? concerning those Thou hast made manifest, or concerning those Thou hast concealed? Wherefore, also, shall I hymn Thee? As if being of myself, as if having something mine own? as being another? For Thou art what I may be, Thou art what I may do, Thou art what I may speak, for Thou art all things, and there is nothing else that Thou art not." *(Ibid.,* pp. 41, 42.)

In all the various exoteric presentations of the Wisdom-Religion, the World-Soul was Intelligence, and was symbolized indifferently in personifications which were male and female, androgyne or sexless; in Egypt and Phœnicia, in Babylon and China, in India and Greece. The Universal Mind of Pythagoras was an attribute of deity universally recognized in antiquity. Athena was Wisdom, and Bacchus the Divine Mind, for the philosopher and initiate. Thus we shall have no difficulty in understanding why Pœmandres is the Mind, and also, by the light of the interpretation of

THE WORLD-SOUL.

the Esoteric Philosophy outlined by H. P. Blavatsky, why there are seven spheres in the Harmony. We must all be musicians and learn to sing sweetly on Apollo's heptachord before we "can hear the powers which are above the eighth nature in a certain sweet voice." We must learn to play on the seven-stringed lute of the radiant Sun-God, and modulate the harmonies of our own septenary nature, for:

"Seven sounding letters sing the praise of me,
 The immortal God, the Almighty Deity;
 Father of all, that cannot wearied be.
 I am the eternal viol of all things,
 Whereby the melody so sweetly rings
 Of heavenly music."

(Oliver, *The Pythagorean Triangle*, p. 175.)

Passing next to the cognate schools of so-called Gnosticism, of those who "tried to know," let us take a thought or two that comes from the minds of the great masters of the Gnôsis.

Epiphanius professes to describe the ceremony whereby the Heracleonitæ prepared a dying brother for the next world. The words of power wherewith the soul might break the seals and burst open the gates of the Nether World in its passage to rest, are given as follows:

"I, the Son from the Father, the Father Preëxisting, but the Son in the present time, am come to behold all things both of others and of my own, and things not altogether of others, but belonging unto Achamôth [one of the aspects of Âkâsha, the World-Soul], who is feminine, and hath created them for herself. But I derive my own origin from the Preëxisting One, and I am going back unto my own from which I have come." (*Adv. Hær.*, xxxvi. 3. *Cf.* also Irenæus, *Adv. Hær.*, I. xxi. 5.)

There were many of such mystic formulæ containing occult truths which students of theosophy will instantly recognize, such as, for instance, the garnering of the harvest of life-experiences by the Higher Ego, quoted by Epiphanius from the lost *Gospel of Philip*, which tells us:

"I have known myself, I have *collected* myself from all parts, neither have I begotten sons unto the Ruler of this World, but I have plucked up the roots, and gathered together the scattered members. I know thee who thou art, for I am one from above." (King's *Gnostics and their Remains*, p. 333.)

But let us take a passing glance at the chief of these great "heresies."

In the system of Simon, the Soul of the World was called Fire (Pûr), as we learn from his *Great Revelation*. (*Philosophumena*, vi. 1.)

Menander, his disciple, called it the (Divine) Thought, Ennoia (Irenæus, *Adv. Hær.*, I. xxiii.) and Satornilus, the disciple of Menander, named it the Unknown Father (Pater Agnôstos). (*Philos.*, vii. 2.)

As we pass down the corridors of history we find the disciple of the latter, Basilîdes, one of the most famous masters of the Gnôsis, re-naming this Un-nameable of many names, and calling it by the mysterious appellation Abraxas, in the transliteration of the mystery-tongue. This was the Unborn Father, Pater Innatus, "He who is not." (Irenæus, *Adv. Hær.*, I. xxiv.; the ἐν τὸ ἀγέννητον, according to Epiphanius, *Adv. Hær.*, XXIV. i.)

This he did for the comprehension of the "many," for the "few" he had a further teaching:

"It was when naught was; nor was that

naught aught of that which is, but (to speak) nakedly, and so as to avoid suspicion, and without any contrivance, It was in fine not even One." *(Philos.,* vii. 1.)

It was, in one of its aspects, the One (1), which is Naught (0), the Perfect Number 10 in the divine manifestation of the " Primary Creation" of the Gods. But even such a metaphysical definition as the above was a materialization to the subtle intellect and spiritual intuition of Basilides, for he says (*ibid.*) :

"That is not absolutely unspeakable which is so called; inasmuch as we call it 'Unspeakable,' but That is not even 'The Unspeakable.' So that That which is not even 'The Unspeakable cannot be named 'The Unspeakable,' for It is beyond all name that can be named."

Carpocrates, who follows next in date, like Satornilus, speaks of the Unknown Father, the Ungenerable, Pater Ingenitus, according to the text of Irenæus. (*Philos.,* viii. 4.)

Finally, the God of the Valentinian Gnôsis was called Bythos, the Depth, from which came all the Æons. This was not called the Father until the primal Syzygy or Double,

THE WORLD-SOUL.

Sigê (Silence), emanated in the All-Unity. This was the Noon of the Egyptians. "Thou art the First-born of the Gods; Thou, from Whom I came forth." "Thou art the One creating Himself," we read in the *Book of the Dead*.

Among prayers to the Supreme Principle are to be remarked the mystic invocations in the Coptic MSS., brought back from Abyssinia, and preserved in the Bodleian Library, Oxford, and in the British Museum. These are treatises on the Egyptian Gnôsis. In the concluding section, the Saviour, the First Mystery, thus addresses the hidden "Father" in the mystic celebration of the initiatory rite of which a fragment remains in the "Sacrament" of the churches. The "prayer" is in the mystery language, untranslatable by the "profane," and runs as follows:

"Hear me, Father, Father of all Fatherhood, Boundless Light! *aeéiouó, iaó, aói, óia, psinóther, thernóps, nópsither, zagouré, pagouré nethmomaóth, nepsiomaóth, marachachtha, thóbarrhabau, tharnachachan, zorokothora, Icou, Sabaóth*." (αεηιονω, ιαω, αωι, ωια, ψινωθερ, θερνωψ, νωψιθερ, ζαγουρη, παγουρη, νεθμομαωθ, νεψιομαωθ, μαραχαχθα, θωβαρ̀ῥαβαν, θαρναχαχαν, ζοροκοθορα, Ιεου, Σαβαωθ.) (Schwartze's *Pistis-Sophia, pag.* 125.)

The theosophical student will at once perceive the method of permutation of the first mystery names, and will remember the seven, five, and three-vowelled names used in the *Secret Doctrine*. Though the full interpretation, however, will probably remain unknown for many a long year to come, from the work itself we learn:

"This is the name of the Immortal $\overline{AAA}$ $\overline{\Omega\Omega\Omega}$;[1] and this is the Name of the Voice which is the Cause of the Motion of the Perfect Man $\overline{III}$."

And again immediately following the invocation we read:

"This is the interpretation thereof: *iota*, the Universe has come forth; *alpha*, they shall return within; *ōō*, there shall be an End of Ends." (*Ibid., pagg.* 357, 358.)

No kabalistic method I have yet applied for obtaining a numerical solution has produced any satisfactory result, except that the sum of the digits of the seven-vowelled name is seven, and the sum of the whole invocation is likewise

[1] "The Father of the Plerôma." *Cf. Notice sur le Papyrus Gnostique Bruce*, M. E. Amélineau, p. 113.

seven. The work has all to be done, and though no theosophist has yet publicly solved the method of this deeply-concealed mysticism, we should bear in mind that no scholar has even attempted a solution other than the wildest speculation bred of a diseased philology.

Let us next take the purely Gnostic teaching of Paul in his first *Letter to the Colossians*. (i. 12-19.)

"Giving thanks to the Father who fits us for a share in the Inheritance of the Holy in the Light; who preserved us from the Power of the Darkness, and translated us into the Kingdom of the Son of his Love, in Whom we have our Redemption,[1] the Remission of Sins, Who is the Image of God, the Invisible, the First-born of every Foundation. For in Him are founded all things, in the Heavens and on Earth, visible and invisible, whether Thrones or Dominions, Rulerships[2] or Powers. All things were founded through Him and for Him. And He is before all, and in Him all things

---

[1] The Authorised Version adds "through his blood," but this is not in the original.

[2] *Archai*, "Beginnings," a Hierarchy of Æons, the same term used in the opening words of the *Gospel according to John*, 'In the Beginning was the Word."

unite (lit., stand together). And He is the Head of the Body of the Assembly,[1] Who is the Beginning,[2] the First-born from the Dead,[3] that He might be in all things Himself supreme. For it seemed good that all the Fullness[4] should dwell in Him."

The spirit and terminology of the whole passage is entirely Gnostic, and can only be understood by a student of Gnosticism. The identity of every Soul with the Over-Soul has been, is, and will be a fundamental doctrine of the Gnôsis. The glorified initiate, the Christ, is the man, who, perfected by the sufferings and consequent experience of many births, finally becomes at one with the Father, the World-Soul, from which he came forth, and at last arises from the Dead; he, indeed, is the first-born, the perfected, self-conscious Mind, or Man, containing in himself the whole divine creation or Plerôma, for he is one with the hierarchies of spiritual Beings who gave him

---

[1] *Ecclesia*, one of the Æons.
[2] *Archê*, the Primæval Æon.
[3] The uninitiated.
[4] *Plerôma*, the totality of the Æons, the synthesis of their Hierarchies. *Cf.* Epiphanius, *Adv. Hær.*, I. iii. 4, who shows the Valentinians quoting this text.

THE WORLD-SOUL.

birth, and instead of being the Microcosm, as when among the Dead, has become the Macrocosm or the World-Soul itself. Through the power of this spiritual union do we win our Redemption from the bonds of matter and thus attain the Remission of Sins, which, according to the wise among the Gnostics, was in the hand of the last and supreme Mystery alone, our own Higher Self, that which is at the same time our Judge and Saviour, sending forth the Sons of its Love, all Rays of the great Ocean of Compassion, into the Darkness of Matter, that Matter may become self-conscious and so perfected. In plainer words, these Rays are each the Higher Ego in every child of the Man (Anthrôpos), proceeding from their Divine Source (Buddhi)—itself that Ocean of Love and Compassion which is the Veil of the Innominable and Incognizable Self (Âtman).

It must not, however, be supposed that such ideas were foreign to the greater minds of Greece and Rome. As has already been said, all that can be attempted in this essay is to select a few passages here and there. Pythagoras and Plato, and the Neoplatonic and Neopythagorean writers, can supply us with innumerable quotations, but as already much has been given from their works in theosophical writings, it will be sufficient to acknowledge the deep debt of gratitude humanity owes these great thinkers, and to show that there are other less known philosophers in this connection who can yield us evidence. For instance, Xenophanes, the principal leader of the Eleatic sect,[1] described God as a Great Being, incomprehensible—

"Incorporeal in substance, and figure globular; and in no respect similar to man. That He is all sight and hearing, but does not breathe. That He is all things; the Mind and Wisdom; not generate but eternal, impassible and immutable." (Oliver, *The Pythagorean Triangle*, 49.)

Lucian also makes Cato say:

"God makes Himself known to all the world; He fills up the whole circle of the Universe, but makes His particular abode in the centre, which is the Soul of the Just." (*Ibid.*, 51.)

Nor were these philosophical concepts

---

[1] αἵρεσις—lit., a school, a heresy: *e.g.*, αἵρεσις Ἑλληνική, a study of Greek literature (Polyb., xl. 6, 3).

THE WORLD-SOUL. 61

evolved by "civilization," for we find the same ideas again and again reiterated in the "Orphic Fragments," which must be given an original antiquity at least contemporaneous with the Trojan War period. Let me here attempt a translation of one of these hymns.

"Zeus is the first. Zeus that rules the thunder is the last. Zeus is the beginning (lit., head). Zeus the middle. From Zeus were all things made. Zeus is male. Zeus, the imperishable, is a maid. Zeus is the foundation of the Earth and starry Heaven. Zeus is the Breath (Air) of all. Zeus the whirl of unwearied Fire. Zeus is the root of the Sea (Water). Zeus is Sun and Moon. Zeus is King. Zeus Himself the Supreme Parent of all. There is but one Power, One Daimôn, One Great Chief of all. One royal frame in which all things circle. Fire, and Water, and Earth, and Æther, Night and Day, and Métis (Wisdom) the first Parent, and all-pleasing Erôs (Love). For all these are in the great body of Zeus. Would'st thou see his head and fair faces? The radiant heaven, round which his golden locks of gleaming stars wave in the space above in all their beauty. On either side two golden taurine horns, the rising and the setting of the Gods, the paths of the celestials. His eyes the Sun and the opposing Moon; His Mind that never lies the imperishable kingly Æther." (From the text of Cory, as found in Eusebius, *Præp. Evan.*, III, Proclus, *Tim.*, and Aristotle, *De Mund.*)

Let us now turn to the lore of our Scandinavian forefathers, to the prose *Edda*, which simply repeats a still more hoary tradition lost in the night of time. Thus it speaks of the World-Soul, of the Supreme Deity and the Primordial State of the Universe:

"Gangler thus began his discourse: 'Who is the first or eldest of the Gods?'

"'In our language,' replied Har, 'He is called Alfadir (All-Father, or the Father of All); but in the old Asgard He had twelve names.'

"'Where is this God?' said Gangler; 'what is His power? and what hath He done to display His glory?'

"'He liveth,' replied Har, 'from all ages, He governeth all realms, and swayeth all things great and small.'

"'He hath formed,' added Jafnhar, 'heaven

THE WORLD-SOUL.

and earth, and the air, and all things thereto belonging.'

"'And what is more,' continued Thridi, 'He hath made man, and given him a soul which shall live and never perish, though the body shall have mouldered away or have been burned to ashes.'

. . . . .

"'But with what did He begin, or what was the beginning of things?' demanded Gangler.

"'Hear,' replied Har, 'what is said in the Völuspá[1]:

> "'Twas time's first dawn,
> When naught yet was,
> Nor sand nor sea,
> Nor cooling wave;
> Earth was not there,
> Nor heaven above.
> Naught save a void
> And yawning gulf."

(From I. A. Blackwell's translation, appended to Bishop Percy's translation of M. Mallet's *Northern Antiquities*, Bohn's Edition, pp. 400, 401.)

---

[1] The Völu or Völo-spá, meaning "The Song of the Prophetess," is a kind of sibylline song containing the whole system of Scandinavian mythology.

And now we have almost done with our serried ranks of witnesses; multitudes have not been called into court, but are waiting if need be to convince the present age that man is of a divine nature and not a congeries of molecules. Let us, therefore, conclude our case by citing from mystical Mohammedan Sufiism, which will tell us why Allah is supreme in the hearts of so many millions of our fellow-men.

The passionate longing for union with the World-Soul, with the Source of our Being, is magnificently portrayed by the mystical Persian poets. Thus Jâmî, in his *Yúsuf ú Zuleykhá*, sings:

"Dismiss every vain fancy, and abandon every doubt;
Blend into One every spirit, and form and place;
See One—know One—speak of One—
Desire One—chant of One—and seek One."

(*Religious Systems of the World*, Art., "Sikhism," p. 306.)

And again:

"In solitude where Being signless dwelt
And all the universe still dormant lay,
Concealed in selflessness, One Being was,
Exempt from 'I' or 'Thou'-ness, and apart

THE WORLD-SOUL.

From all duality; Beauty Supreme,
Unmanifest, except unto Itself
By Its own light, yet fraught with power to charm
The souls of all; concealed in the Unseen,
An Essence pure, unstained by aught of ill."

(Ibid., p. 328.)

Perhaps some may be surprised that I have omitted from the numerous citations already adduced any reference to Buddhism. I have done so, not because the idea of the World-Soul is absent from that system, but because, for the most part, it is difficult to find therein anything in the nature of prayers or adoration to a Supreme Principle. The protest of Gautama against the externalization of the Divine was so strong, that his followers, as it seems to me, have in course of time leaned to extremes, and preferred to express their aspirations rather in terms of denial of material qualities than in positive terms of definition of spiritual attributes. But what after all is Nirvâna but a synonym of the World-Soul? And this is well shown by the more transcendent term Parinirvâna, which provides for infinite extension of the concept.

The word *nir-vâna* means literally "blown

out," "extinguished," as of a fire; but it also means "tamed," as, for instance, *a-nirvâna*, used of an elephant, not tamed, or one just caught or wild. There is no doubt whatever that the term describes a state in which the lower nature is entirely tamed, though it is to be regretted that a more positive teaching does not obtain in the so-called Southern Church of Buddhism. Its greatest metaphysicians, however, declare that the state of Nirvâna is of such a nature that no words can even hint at its reality, much less describe it, and that it is not wise to inculcate material ideas, however lofty, in the minds of the people. Therefore it is that in popular Buddhism we are met with such apparently self-contradictory statements as:

"They who, by steadfast mind, have become exempt from evil desire, and well-trained in the teachings of Gautama; they, having obtained the fruit of the fourth Path, and immersed themselves in that ambrosia, have received without price, and are in the enjoyment of Nirvâna. Their old Karma is exhausted, no new Karma is being produced; their hearts are free from the longing after future life; the cause of their existence being destroyed, and no new yearnings springing up within them, they, the wise, are extinguished like this lamp." *(Ratana Sutta,* 7, 14.*)*

One naturally asks: If they are extinguished, how can they enjoy Nirvâna? But such contradictions are the lot of all popular presentations of religion, and in fact, it seems to be in the nature of things that Truth can only be stated in a paradox. Nothing but a study of esotericism will reconcile the exoteric systems with each other and with themselves; nor will anything else persuade an orthodox Buddhist that there is salvation without the "teachings of Gautama," or a Brâhman without the Vedas, or a Christian without the Bible. How different is the spirit that animates some among the Lamas, who consider it a sin, not only to say, but even to think, that their religion is superior to that of any other man!

Let me then venture on a positive exposition among all this over-cautious negation, and suggest that the Nirvânic state is the plane of consciousness of the World-Soul. Of course this is not orthodox Buddhism, either of the Northern or Southern Church, as known to us, but it enables us to reconcile Buddhism with the other world systems, and also to see how the esoteric interpretation is the connecting link between all of them, and how it completes their insufficient statements.

The "great heresy" of the "pilgrim soul" is the feeling of "separateness." With men, the senses, and especially the brain-mind, is that which keeps us from the rest, for they produce the illusion of an *external* universe, whereas it is the heart that binds us to our fellows, and which alone can make us one with all men and with all nature. And though I do not wish to fall into the error of transferring our present conditions to that of the World-Soul, and thus becoming guilty of materializing and anthropomorphizing that which transcends our present consciousness, still I think that the suggestion of an analogy may not be harmful. As in man the head externalizes and separates, and the heart binds and looks within, so, I would imagine, there is an external state of consciousness of the World-Soul, and also an internal consciousness. Thus we find a "head-doctrine" and a "heart-doctrine" in every religion, and a goal that can be reached by pursuing either. Nirvâna can be reached by two Paths. By one an external state of consciousness can be arrived at, by the other a union with "all that lives and breathes." Of course, the external state mentioned is one internal and subjective to our present senses, but it differs from that full reality of the heart that beats in compassion with all hearts, just as the gratification of the senses and intellect differs from the calm of a noble soul conscious of striving for truth and purity in the midst of the most unfavourable surroundings.

Nor is the intuition of the heart doctrine absent from any of the best religionists of to-day. The most advanced thinkers of Christendom utterly reject the idea of an eternal joy in Heaven, spent in vain adoration and inactive bliss. With true intuition they conceive that the joy of Heaven would be incomplete so long as others suffer. The grim Calvinism of a Tertullian who counted it one of the joys of his Heaven to look down upon the tortures of the damned in Hell, finds approbation only among the ignorant. The larger minds of the Church will have none of it, just as some Buddhists count the Pratyeka Buddha, he who obtains the Nirvâna of the "eye," a symbol of spiritual selfishness. For like as the "spooks" in a *séance*-room rejoice to masquerade as great characters, and call themselves Homer, and Dante, and Jesus, so do countless religionists love to call themselves Christians and Buddhists, whereas they have as little claim to the title as the irresponsible "spooks."

To me, then, the attainment of Nirvâna, or the "Peace of God," or Moksha (Liberation), or whatever name you choose to call it by, is the attainment of the degree of consciousness of the World-Soul. For although I have referred it to Heaven as an illustration, I would rather connote this with Svarga or Devachan, or whatever name is given to the state of bliss between two earth-lives. But this is not *becoming* the World-Soul, or a World-Soul, any more than the possession of a human body constitutes an entity a *man*. To become the World-Soul, the Nirvâna of the "eye" must be renounced, just as the world of external sensation must be renounced to become one with the Higher Ego, who commands: "Leave all that thou hast, and follow *Me*," in that "ye brought nothing into the world, neither shall ye take anything out."

THE WORLD-SOUL. 71

Nirvâna must be renounced; for until every Soul of man has attained Nirvâna, the World-Soul has no rest, and he who would be one with it must take up the burden of a like responsibility; and just as the adept purifies the atoms of his body from the taint of passion in order to reach the knowledge of the Self, so must the Nirmânakâya aid in purifying the souls, whose purification will enable that World-Soul to ascend to a more glorious state of activity. And though we make these distinctions in order to give some faint idea of the mystery, still all is the Self sacrificing Itself to Itself, and selfishness and selflessness are words that lose their meanings in an intuition that escapes all words.

But to return to popular Buddhism. Though there is little evidence of any cult of a Supreme Principle, in the ordinary sense of the word, in the Southern Church, in the Northern Church it is different. The cult of one or other of the Bodhisattvas is extensively practised, if we are to depend upon the authorities: and we find prayers addressed to Manjushrî, the personification of Wisdom, and to Avalokiteshvara, the "merciful protector and preserver of the world and of men," who are invoked and prayed to as, for example, by Fa Hian (*Buddhism*, by T. W. Rhys Davids, p. 203) just as Shiva or Vishnu is worshipped by orthodox Hindus.

How the esoteric interpretation throws light on the misunderstanding of the exoteric rituals, students of the Esoteric Philosophy know from the works of H. P. Blavatsky; and the World-Soul, Âdi-Buddha, which emanates the five (according to the Esoteric Philosophy, seven) Dhyâni-Buddhas, shows the identity of conception with the other great religions.

Perhaps it may also have caused surprise that the Upanishads have not been cited; but that has not been for lack of passages, for the whole object of these mystical scriptures is to inculcate the identity of man with the All. This is the key-note of the Âryan religion, and every Upanishad persistently reiterates it. As H. P. Blavatsky, but for whose teaching these essays would not have been written, says in that inexhaustable store-house of instruction, and information, *The Secret Doctrine* (i. 330):

"Not till the Unit is merged in the All, whether on this or any other plane, and Subject

THE WORLD-SOUL.

and Object alike vanish in the absolute negation of the Nirvânic State (negation, only from *our* plane), not until then is scaled that peak of Omniscience—the knowledge of things-in-themselves; and the solution of the yet more awful riddle approached, before which even the highest Dhyân Chohan must bow in silence and ignorance—the unspeakable mystery of That which is called by the Vedântins, Parabrahman."

Of course this may be denied by the theist, but remember that definition, even of the most metaphysical character, will land the definer in the most preposterous contradictions. The reader may also object: what does Madame Blavatsky know of the highest Dhyân Chohan (Spiritual Existence)? To which, if I may venture to say so, her reply would be, as it has been to many another question: "Thus have I heard." In other words, the teaching is that of those whom H. P. Blavatsky knew had knowledge. But that is not all; for the explanations contained in *The Secret Doctrine* were never meant to rest on mere assertion, and the statement above quoted finds its support in all the great world-religions, as may be amply seen even from the few quotations adduced in this article.

I have also, it will be remarked, avoided any selections from the heterogeneous Scriptures which are now called the Old Testament, preferring to give citations from the Kabalah. Perhaps also some readers may be surprised that I have also refrained from giving the prayer of Christendom from the New Testament, commonly known as the "Lord's Prayer." But my reason for this is that it was not a Christian prayer originally, but a Jewish one, and that even James, the "brother of the Lord," gives a teaching directly opposed to one of its principal clauses. This prayer is found almost *verbatim* in the Jewish Kadish, and runs as follows :

"Our Father, which art in heaven, be gracious to us, O Lord our God; hallowed be Thy name; and let the remembrance of Thee be glorified in heaven above, and upon earth here below. Let Thy kingdom reign over us, now and for ever. Thy holy men of old said : 'Remit and forgive unto all men whatsoever they have done against me.' And lead us not into temptation, but deliver us from the evil

THE WORLD-SOUL.

thing. For Thine is the Kingdom, and Thou shalt reign in glory, for ever and for ever more.[1]

Moreover if James is any authority, we find ourselves placed on the horns of a theological dilemma, for he says:

"Let no one, when he is tempted, say 'I am tempted of the Deity': for the Deity cannot be tempted of evil, neither tempteth he any man."[2]

A teaching more in harmony with the direction to "enter into *thy* closet, and when thou hast shut *thy* door pray to *thy Father in secret.*" (*Matthew* vi. 6, τῷ πατρί σου τῷ ἐν τῷ κρυπτῷ.) This does not mean that being in a physical closet, the prayer is thus "in secret." But that this prayer, or contemplation, is to be made to, or on, the "Father in Secret," within the "chamber of the heart," as the Greek text proves beyond any question.

And now, in closing, let me again say that I

---

[1] Gerald Massey, *The Natural Genesis*, ii. 469. Version from *A Critical Examination of the Gospel History*, p. 109. *Cf.* Basnage, *Hist. des Juifs*, p. 374.

[2] *James*, i. 13. The words used for tempted, etc., are all from the verb πειράζομαι, and are identical with the word used in the prayer as found in the texts of *Matthew* (vi. 13) and *Luke* (xi. 4), viz., πειρασμός.

think that both the believers in a Personal God and those who refuse to give any attribute to Deity may find some common ground of agreement in the concept of the World-Soul. Of course, it is only to the broad-minded that any appeal is made.

In our days unorthodoxy is no longer a term of reproach; it has now securely saddled reproach on the back of orthodoxy. And for this desirable state of affairs we owe many thanks to fearless free thought, to the unwinking scrutiny of scientific observation, and the logic of scientific methods. But the pendulum begins to swing to the extreme, and it is time to protest against freedom developing into licence, and the newly-fashioned idols of orthodox science being substituted for the crumbling idols of orthodox religion. Religious thinkers are beginning to broaden in every direction, and though Churchmen still hold persistently to the term " Personal " God, which owes its genesis to an ignorant blunder, they will, under pressure, so sublimate the concept that it is easy to perceive that the words have no longer for them their just meaning, and that for some reason best known to themselves, or for some undefined fear, or conservative policy, they prefer to call white black. The theist contends that men must have something to lean on, and that to take away the personality of Deity would be to destroy the hope of the Christian world. But why so? Is there not a Christ in every man to lean upon? Nay, is not the Christ the very Man himself, if he would but know *Himself?* What more is requisite?

But the orthodox world has so long been reciting invocations to Jehovah that they have forgotten the teachings of their Founder who spoke of the "Father in Secret"—no new teaching, as the above quotations amply prove, but a repetition of the old, old mystery. And yet the more advanced Christians are almost invariably ashamed of Jehovah and do not care to have his exploits referred to. They try to explain it by airily referring to a partial revelation to the Jews, preluding a full revelation to themselves. If you refer to the injustice of leaving other world-religions out in the cold, they generally maintain a freezing silence and regard you henceforward as a dangerous disturber of the public morals. Or they will talk of monotheism and polytheism, and beg the question by assuming that Judaism, in its present dead-letter orthodox garb, is monotheism, whereas in reality it should rather be called monolatry.

No doubt some who read this and call themselves Christians, will see here an additional reason for condemning theosophical writers as anti-Christian, and in disgust will inform their friends that theosophy is an enemy of Christ and a child of that interesting creation of the human brain which is called the Devil. And perhaps they are partially right from their own point of view, for it certainly is destructive of *their* dogmas and superstitions; but whether such dogmas and superstitions were taught by the Christ is another question.

But equally so is theosophy destructive of dogmas and superstitions in Brâhmanism, or Buddhism, or Taoism, or Mohammedanism, and so to the bigoted externalist of each of these religions it must be anti-Brâhmanical, anti-Buddhistic, and so on. Whereas the theosophist claims that he is not really an enemy of any religion, but, on the contrary, as true a believer as any of such religionists.

In such a pitiable state of affairs, our task

should be to bring once more to the sight of men the old ideals of humanity, trusting that the memory of the past may come back once more, and that all men, without distinction of race, caste, creed or sex, may recognize a common possession in them. And may they weld us together in those bonds of harmony and brotherhood which have only been loosed by licence, but which freedom will once more place on our willing hands!

*Vâsânsi jîrnâni yathâ vihâya
Navâni grihnâti naro 'parâni
Tathâ sharîrâni vihâya jîrnâny—
Anyâni sanyâti navâni dehî.*

As a man casting off worn-out garments takes other new ones, so the lord of the body casting off worn-out bodies enters other new ones.—

BHAGAVAD GÎTÂ, ii. 22.

THE VESTURES OF THE SOUL.

HANDBOOKS and pamphlets on theosophy—as sketched in the system of the Esoteric Philosophy that has been so prominently brought forward by H. P. Blavatsky—are to-day so numerous, that almost all my readers must be aware of what have been called the seven "principles" of man. That is to say, that man is regarded from seven points of view, although in reality he is ever one entity. This has been done, in order that we may get a clearer idea of the complex nature of the vehicles, sheaths, garments, or vestures, in which the divine consciousness manifests itself in the case of the human being. For as in all sciences, so in the greatest science of all—that of the human soul—we must resort to analysis, if we would have a clear conception of the problem before us.

There are many systems, all of which divide

the nature of man, each in its own way. In the present essay, however, I shall not insist on any precise division, but shall endeavour to give you some idea of what some of these soul-vestures may be. And by Soul I mean the divine consciousness in man—which is spoken of sometimes as the Self—and not the restricted idea that is more generally connoted with the term in the western world. Of this Self, the *Bhagavad Gîtâ* speaks as follows (ii. 20):

"This is not born, nor dies it ever, nor having once been will it not be again. Unborn, eternal, everlasting, ancient, this is not slain though the body be slain."

Aye, no matter how sublime and god-like the body or vesture may be— for even that garment of God by which men behold Him, as Goethe says, the whole conceivable universe, woven in the loom of time, even this will perish in the eternities. But the Self is (*ibid.*, ii. 24.):

"Eternal, all-pervading, stable, immovable, ancient—this is said to be the unmanifestable, this the unthinkable, this the unchangeable."

Therefore, as Krishna says:

"Knowing it to be such, pray do not grieve."

Yes, the Soul has many a garment besides

the "coats of skin" that covered the spiritual nakedness of our primeval Selves, in the childhood of our present humanity. It was left to the dulled intellect of our present age and its immediate predecessors to clothe the naked physical bodies of a pictorial Adam and Eve with the skins of wild beasts, stitched together, forsooth, by the "Lord God" himself. It is high time to end such a theological farce and publish a revised edition of this grand soul-myth, which, if Carlyle had not anticipated us, we might very appropriately call the "sartor resartus," or stitcher re-stitched. Let us first trace the descent of the Soul, or Self, as it involves downwards, clothing itself in several main vestures and other minor ones, according to the teaching of the Vedântic philosophers and seers of ancient India. You will find the passage in that mystical treatise, *The Dream of Râvan*, (London: The Theosophical Publishing Society, 1895). The "Four States and Tabernacles of Man" are described as follows:

"There are four spheres of existence, one enfolding the other[1]—(1) the inmost sphere of

---

[1] That is to say, interpenetrating each other, and not like the skins of the onion.

Turîya [lit., the fourth], in which the individualized spirit lives the ecstatic life;[1] (2) the sphere of transition, or Lethe, in which the spirit, plunged in the ocean of Agñâna [non-wisdom] or total unconsciousness;[2] and utterly forgetting its real Self,[3] undergoes a change of gnostic tendency [polarity?] ;[4] and from not knowing at all, or absolute unconsciousness, emerges on the hither side of that Lethean boundary to a false or reversed knowledge of things (Viparîta Gñâna), under the influence of an illusive Prâgña, or belief in, and tendency to, knowledge *outward* from itself, in which delusion it thoroughly believes, and now endeavours to realize: whereas the true knowledge which it had in the state of Turîya, or the ecstatic life, was all *within* itself, in which it intuitively knew and experienced all things. And from the sphere of Prâgña, or out-knowing—this struggle to reach and recover *outside* itself all that it once possessed *within* itself, and lost—

---

[1] On its own plane of true spiritual consciousness.

[2] As we know consciousness.

[3] Because of this vesture of Agñâna.

[4] That is to say of *recovering* its primal wisdom or Gñâna, which is the same word as Gnôsis.

to regain for the lost intuition an objective perception through the senses and understanding—in which the spirit became an intelligence—it merges into (3) the third sphere of dreams, where it believes in a universe of light and shade, and where all existence is in the way of Â-bhâsa, or phantasm. There it imagines itself into the Lingadeha (Psyche)[1] or subtle, semi-material, ethereal, soul, composed of a vibrating or knowing pentad, and a breathing or undulating pentad. The vibrating or knowing pentad consists of simple consciousness radiating into four different forms of knowledge—*(a)* the egoity or consciousness of self; *(b)* the ever-changing, devising, wishing mind, imagination or fancy; *(c)* the thinking, reflecting, remembering faculty; and *(d)* the apprehending and determining understanding or judgment.[2]

"The breathing or undulating pentad contains the five vital auræ—namely, the breath of life, and the four nervous æthers that produce

---

[1] This is the Astral Soul, not the Astral Body of the Esoteric Philosophy.

[2] This is the Lower Mind or Manas of the Esoteric Philosophy, and the Antahkarana or Inner Organ of the Vedântins, consisting of *(a)* Ahankâra, *(b)* Chittam, *(c)* Manas, *(d)* Buddhi.

sensation, motion, and the other vital phenomena.

"From this subtle personification and phantasmal sphere, in due time it progresses into (4) the fourth or outmost sphere, where matter and sense are triumphant; where the universe is believed a solid reality; where all things exist in the mode of Â-kâra,[1] substantial form; and where that—which successively forgot itself from spirit into absolute unconsciousness and awoke on this side of that boundary of oblivion into an intelligence struggling outward, and from this outward struggling intelligence imagined itself into a conscious, feeling, breathing, nervous soul, prepared for further clothing—where that which does all this now out-realises itself from soul into a body, with five senses or organs of perception, and five organs of action, to suit it for knowing and acting in the external world, which it once held within, but has now wrought out of itself.[2]

---

[1] From *â-kri*, to bring towards or down, to make or form wholly.

[2] The five organs of sensation are the skin, eyes, nose, ears, tongue, corresponding to the simple consciousness and the four different forms of knowledge of the vibrating or knowing pentad, *viz.*, the Lower Mind. The five organs of action

(1) The first or spiritual state was ecstasy; (2) from ecstasy it forgot itself into deep sleep; (3) from profound sleep it awoke out of unconsciousness, but still within itself, into the internal world of dreams; (4) from dreaming it passed finally into the thoroughly waking state, and the outer world of sense. Each state has an embodiment of ideas or language of its own. (1) The universal, eternal, ever-present intuitions that be eternally with the spirit in the first, are in the second utterly forgotten for a time, and (2) then emerge reversed, limited, and translated into divided successive intellections, or gropings, rather, of a struggling and as yet unorganized intelligence, having reference to place and time, and an external historical world, which it seeks but cannot all at once realize outside itself. In the third (3) they become pictured by a creative fantasy into phantasms of persons, things and events, in a world of light and shade within us, which is visible even when the eyes are sealed in dreaming

are the mouth, hands, feet, and the two lower organs, corresponding to the breath of life and the four nervous æthers, which are the five vital auræ of the breathing or undulating pentad.

slumber, and is a prophecy and forecast shadow of the solid world that is coming. In the fourth (4) the out-forming or objectivity is complete. They are embodied by the senses into hard external realities in a world without us. That ancient seer (Kavi Purâna) which the *Gîtâ* and *Mahâbhârata* mention as abiding in the breast of each, is (1) first a prophet and poet; then (2) he falls asleep and awakes as a blindfold logician and historian, without materials for reasoning, or a world for events, but groping towards them; next (3) a painter with an ear for inward phantasmal music, too; at last (4) a sculptor carving out hard palpable solidities."

I have ventured on this lengthy quotation because it is one of the plainest statements I have yet found of the famous but difficult system of Vedântic psychology. It has to be carefully thought out to be fully appreciated, but will well repay the trouble by bringing to light many fresh beauties which a cursory first reading will necessarily slur over. It is a most beautiful idea, that of the self-same Self being successively clothed in Vestures which transform it first into a poet and prophet, in a state out of time and space; then a blindfold logician and historian, in time and space, in a sort of external historical world, with which it is not yet in touch, and where its operations are compared to divided successive intellections or gropings; next a painter and musician limning images on the phantasmal surface of things, and with an ear for inward harmony; and lastly a sculptor, carving out objects in three dimensional space.

As may be seen from the above, the four, or rather three states—for it would be wrong to term the highest a state, in that it represents the Self in its own essence—correspond to the three great Vestures of the Soul, and we are told that an adept can separate them one from another, and clothe the Self in which he will.

These Vestures are again composed of several Garments, which are generally spoken of as Sheaths (Koshas). Starting from below, we have first the Food Sheath, formed from food by the alchemy of nature. This is transformed by the vital auræ into protoplasm, and so transformed into blood, flesh, bone, muscle, skin, etc., eventuating finally into our physical body —truly graphically described as a "coat of skin."

This is called the Food Garment or Sheath (Anna-maya Kosha).[1] Next we have the fivefold Garment of the life breath, the undulating pentad, for it energises in long rhythmic waves. This is called the Life Sheath (Prâna-maya Kosha). Following this comes the Garment of the vibrating pentad whose wave lengths are shorter and more rapid, for thought is more rapid than even the life forces in the body. This latter Garment is twofold: one Sheath being connected with determination, understanding and judgment; the other with the faculty which refers all things to what we call "ourselves"—our illusive personalities—with the ever-changing, devising, wishing mind, imagination, or fancy, and the thinking, expecting, remembering faculty. No doubt a clearer definition could be made, but the traditional method of the Vedântic schools has based its classification on

---

[1] I should, however, like to be informed why the modern Vedântic classification omits the Anna-*rasa*-maya Kosha, which, in the second Anuvâka of *Taittiriyopanishad*, is given as entirely distinct from either the Anna-maya or Prâna-maya Kosha. The Sheath composed of the essence (*rasa*) of food should correspond with the Linga Sharîra of the Esoteric Philosophy.

VESTURES OF THE SOUL.

the five developed senses, and publicly ignores the septenary division, which alone can provide a truly scientific classification. But as the purpose of this present paper is not to criticize but to give some idea of the Garments of the Soul, we will proceed. The two Garments just referred to are called the Mind and Knowledge Sheaths (Mano-maya and Vi-gñâna-maya Koshas). And above them is that Lethean Vesture which, though it may prevent us from knowing our true Selves as long as we identify ourselves with our temporary Garments, is nevertheless a blessed vesture of forgetfulness of the misery and shame of our past lives, when we once more don it and enter into the much needed rest from our labours. This has thus been appropriately termed the Garment of Bliss (Ânanda-maya Kosha).

But all our misery consists in our imagining ourselves apart from the Self. And to destroy this misery we must begin by freeing ourselves from the illusion of mistaking these various Garments for our real Selves. This must be done gradually, beginning with the lowest, the Food Garment.

The illusion I refer to is stated in such false

ideas as :[1] I am a male ; I am a female ; I am born ; I live ; I grow ; I change ; I decay ; I shall hereafter die ; I am a child, a youth, an old man ; I am a priest, a physician, a tradesman ; a total abstainer, a drunkard.

Again the illusion of identifying oneself with the Life Garment is revealed by such thoughts as : I am hungry ; I am thirsty ; I am strong ; I am brave ; I am the talker, the walker, the giver ; I am dumb, I am lame.

So again with the Mind Garment, by such conceptions as : I am one that thinks, or fancies, or grieves, or am deluded ; I am the hearer, toucher, the taster and he who smells ; I am deaf, or blind.

And then with the Garment of Knowledge or Discrimination, by such thoughts as : I am intelligent ; I am going to Heaven ; I am a learned person ; I am indifferent to sensual pleasures.

And so finally with the Garment of Bliss, by thinking : I am happy ; I am content ; I am ignorant or vicious ; I am wise ; I am foolish.

---

[1] I have adapted the following from the translation of the "Meditations of Vâsudeva"—*Lucifer*, September, 1892, pp. 24 *et seqq.*, now also published in book form.

The last example must be taken as the reflection of the characteristics of this Garment in the embodied state. When freed from the body, this Garment is freed from the idea of what we call the " I."

Again, the very same ideas, though with a different nomenclature, are to be found in the books of wisdom, of ancient Egypt. Let us select a few passages from the *Divine Pymander* of Hermes Trismegistus, which still retains some of the old ideas, no matter how garbled by translation, re-translation and mis-translation. In the Fourth Book called " The Key," we read (Everard's Translation, pp. 25 *et seqq.*) :

" 46. But the Soul of Man is carried in this manner : The Mind is in Reason, Reason in the Soul, The Soul in the Spirit, The Spirit in the Body."

That is to say the Soul of Man, or the Self, is clothed : first with the Blissful Garment of Mind ; then with the Knowing Garment of Reason ; then with the Garment of Fancy and the rest, called by Hermes the Soul ; next with the Garment of Life or Spirit ; and last of all by the Gross Body. For as Hermes says :

"47. The Spirit [*i.e.*, Life or Prána] being diffused and going through the veins, and arteries, and blood, both moveth the living creature, and after a certain manner beareth it.

"48. Wherefore some also have thought the Soul to be blood, being deceived in Nature, not knowing that first the Spirit must return into the Soul, and then the blood is congealed, and the veins and arteries emptied, and then the living thing dieth : and this is the death of the Body."

And further on he says, speaking of the change which takes place at death :

"56. When the Soul [or Lower Mind] runs back into itself, the Spirit is contracted into the blood, and the Soul into the Spirit. But the Mind [Higher Mind] being made pure, and free from these clothings, and being Divine by Nature, taking a Fiery Body [or Vesture],[1] rangeth abroad in every place, leaving the Soul to judgment and to the punishment it hath deserved."

This refers to the post-mortem state of the

---

[1] This will explain the mystical meaning of the "chariot of fire," in which Elijah is carried to Heaven, and much else.

cast-off lower Garments which endure for a time in a state which the Esoteric Philosophy calls Kâma Loka or the Place of Desire. Further on again Hermes speaks more distinctly of these Garments when he says :

"59. The disposition of these Clothings or Covers is done in an Earthly Body; for it is impossible that the Mind [the Higher] should establish or rest itself, naked, and of itself in an Earthly Body; neither is the Earthly Body able to bear such immortality: and, therefore, that it might suffer so great virtue, the Mind compacted, as it were, and took to itself the passable Body of the Soul [Lower Mind] as a Covering or Clothing. And the Soul being also in some sort Divine, useth the Spirit [Prâna] as her Minister or Servant; and the Spirit governeth the living things [that is to say, the Body which is composed of myriads of 'lives'].

"60. When therefore the Mind is separated, and departeth from the Earthly Body, presently it puts on its Fiery Coat, which it could not do, having to dwell in an Earthly Body.

"61. For the Earth cannot suffer Fire, for it is all burned of a small spark; therefore is the Water poured round about the Earth, as a wall or defence, to withstand the flame of Fire. [That is to say, the Physical Body is first of all clad in an Astral Garment or Body.]

"62. But the Mind being the most sharp or swift of all the Divine Cogitations, and more swift than all the Elements, hath the Fire for its Body.

"63. For the Mind, which is the Workman of all, useth the Fire as his Instrument in his Workmanship; and he that is the Workman of all useth it to the making of all things, as it is used by Man to the making of Earthly things only. For the Mind that is upon Earth [the Lower Mind], void or naked of Fire, cannot do the business of men, nor that which is otherwise the affairs of God.

"64. But the Soul of Man [the Lower Manas, the Ray from the Higher Mind], and yet not every one, but that which is pious and religious, is Angelic and Divine. And such a Soul, after it is departed from the Body, having striven the strife of Piety, becomes either Mind or God.

"65. And the strife of Piety is to know God [the Self], and to injure no Man; and this way it becomes Mind.

"66. But the impious Soul abideth in its own offence, punished of itself, and seeking an Earthly and Human Body to enter into.

"67. For no other Body is capable of a Human Soul, neither is it lawful for a Man's Soul to fall into the Body of an unreasonable living thing: For it is the Law or Decree of God to preserve a Human Soul from so great a contumely and reproach."

Here we have an unbroken ray of light shining out of the darkness from the Mysteries of Ancient Egypt. The secret teaching of the temples differed entirely from the popular superstition; and though the populace were taught that they risked to be reincarnated in the bodies of animals, in order that fear might generate virtue, the better instructed were taught the higher doctrine. The same obtains unconsciously in Christianity to-day. Hell for the ignorant, a more enlightened teaching for those who can understand.

In the collection of heterogeneous books, commonly known as the Bible, the persistent mistranslation of purely technical terms has resulted in a simple trichotomy of man into Body, Soul and Spirit, which is in itself insufficient to represent the thought of the writers of the several books. For instance, Paul, in his *First Letter to the Corinthians* (ch. xv), says that every seed has its appropriate body, that there are many kinds of " Fleshes," and also Heavenly and Earthly Bodies (σώματα ἐπουράνια, καὶ σώματα ἐπίγεια). In this connection he speaks of the Bodies of the Sun, Moon and Stars which he calls " Glories " (δόξαι), and which we may compare with the " Fiery Vesture " mentioned by Hermes—Sidereal Bodies, to use the words of Paracelsus. Later on he speaks of a Psychic and Pneumatic, or Spiritual, Body (εἰ ἔστι σῶμα ψυχικόν, ἔστι καὶ πνευματικόν), in connection with which he says that the " first birth " is into a Living Soul (ψυχὴν ζῶσαν), whereas the " second birth " will be into a Vivifying Spirit (πνεῦμα ζωποιοῦν). The " first man " is said to be of the earth, or rather of liquid earth, and hence called " choïc "—reminding us of the Gnostic fourfold division into Choïc, Hylic, Psychic and Pneumatic Bodies, but difficult to sort out from the Paulinian text as it stands. Further on we read of the " image " of the Choïc Man and of the " image " of the Heavenly Man, purely technical terms again. It was in one of these Bodies that this Initiate was wrapt to the Third Heaven,[1] which Heavens—no matter how many so ever they be—have each an appropriate Vesture of Purity. And there he heard those "ineffable words" (ἄρρητα ῥήματα) which cannot be spoken; they can no more be expressed in human speech than can the ocean be contained in a water pot.

What the learned Gnostics and Kabalists taught concerning the "coats of skins" of our allegorical First Parents in the mystical Garden of Eden I have already told you, but in order that the idea may not rest merely on my assertion, here is one out of many passages from their books. It is taken from the *Zohar*, the kabalistic "Book of Splendour" (ii. 229*b*; quoted in Mackenzie's *Royal Masonic Cyclopædia*, p. 411):

"When Adam dwelled in the Garden of Eden, he was dressed in the celestial garment which is a garment of heavenly light. But when he was expelled from the Garden of Eden, and became subject to the wants of this world, what is written? 'The Lord God [Elohim]

---

[1] II. *Corinthians*, xii. 2.

made coats of skins unto Adam and to his wife, and clothed them' (*Gen.*, iii. 21), for prior to this they had garments of light—light of that light which was used in the Garden of Eden."

For as the *Zohar* says elsewhere (ii. 76a; *ibid.*, p. 412):

"The mystery of the earthly man is after the mystery of the Heavenly Man. And just as we see in the firmament above, covering all things, different signs which are formed of the stars and planets, and which contain secret things and profound mysteries, studied by those who are wise and expert in those signs ; so these are in the skin [Astral Body rather] which is the cover of the body of the son of man, and which is like the sky which covers all things, signs, and features, which are the stars and planets of the skin, indicating secret things and profound mysteries."

There is a curious Rabbinical tradition with regard to these "coats of skins" which may not be without interest, if quoted in this connection. It is found in the *Yaschar* or *Sepher Haiyaschar*, "The Book of the Just," more commonly known as "The Book of the Generations of Adam" or "The Book of the History of Man " which has been translated into French by the Chevalier P. L. B. Drach. The legend runs as follows (see Migne, *Dictionnaire des Apocryphes*, tom. ii. coll. 1102, 1150) :

"After the death of Adam and Eve, these coats were given to Enoch, son of Jared. Enoch, at the time of his being taken to God, gave them to his son Mathusalah. After the death of Mathusalah, Noah took them and kept them with him in the Ark. Ham stole them and hid them so successfully that his brethren were unable to find them. Ham gave them secretly to his eldest son Chus, who made a mystery of it to his brothers and sons. When Nimrod reached the age of twenty years, he (Chus) clothed him with this vesture, which gave him extraordinary strength."

It was only when Nimrod was stripped of this garment that he could be killed.

We have all heard of Joseph's "coat of many colours" (*Genesis*, xxxvii. 3)— $\chi\iota\tau\widehat{\omega}\nu\alpha$ $\pi o\iota\kappa\iota\lambda o\nu$, as the Septuagint translation has it—but few have any idea that this is a symbolical Garment of the Soul, woven of a warp and woof of beams from the Spiritual Sun, just as the prismatic rays originate from a physical beam of sunlight.

Such again is the Garment that all must be clothed in when the King Initiate comes in to inspect the guests, as we are told in the *Gospel according to Matthew* (xxii. 11.). This "wedding garment" (ἔνδυμα γάμου) is no mortal dress, but a Garment of the Soul, a very real Vesture that we have to weave for ourselves. It must be "a coat (χιτών) . . . . without seam, woven from the top throughout" (*John*, xix. 23), the same which Joseph's Brethren brought back to his Father (Âtmâ) when they had sold the Beloved Son (Manas) into the slavery of incarnation in the Egypt of the body, and for which the soldiers cast lots when the Christ is crucified.

This is a very old story, but its interpretation is as old as the story itself, for I am simply repeating what the sages of old taught their disciples. And this brings me towards the completion of my task where I would try to convey to you some slight idea of the three Great Vestures of Initiation which correspond to the three higher Principles of Man according to the classification of the Esoteric Philosophy. In that marvellous relic of Gnostic Philosophy called the *Pistis-Sophia* (see *Lucifer*,

April, 1890, p. 111, and June, 1890, pp. 321, 322), the three vestures of the Glorified Christos or perfected man—what we may all be in some future birth—are thus described :

"And the Disciples saw not Jesus because of the great Light with which he was surrounded, or which proceeded from him. For their eyes were darkened because of it. But they gazed upon the Light only, shooting forth great rays of light. Nor were the rays equal to one another, and the Light was of divers modes and various aspect, from the lower to the higher part thereof, each ray more admirable than its fellow in infinite manner, in the great radiance of the immeasurable Light. It stretched from the earth to the heaven. . . . It was of three degrees, one surpassing the other in infinite manner. The second, which was in the midst, excelled the first which was below it, and the third, the most admirable of all, surpassed the other twain."

The Master explains this mystery to his Disciples as follows :

"Rejoice, therefore, in that the time is come that I should put on my Vesture.

"Lo! I have put on my Vesture and all

power has been given me by the First Mystery. Yet a little while and I will tell you every Mystery and every Completion; henceforth from this hour I will conceal naught from you, but in Perfectness will I perfect you in all Completion, and all Perfectioning and every Mystery, which indeed are the End of all Ends, and the Completion of all Completions, and the Wisdom (Gnôsis) of all Wisdoms. Hearken! I will tell you all things which have befallen me.

"It came to pass, when the sun had risen in the places of the East, a great Stream of Light descended, in which was my Vesture, which I placed in the Four-and-twentieth Mystery. And I found the Mystery on my Vesture written in Five Words, which pertain to the Height. ZAMA ZAMA OZZA RACHAMA ÔZAI.[1] And this is the inter-

---

[1] Compare the Pancha-Kosha or Five Sheaths of the Vedântins previously referred to. For an explanation of the number *five*, and the pentagon, see *Secret Doctrine*, ii. pp. 575-580. In one of the books of the Peratæ Gnostics mention is made of a dodecagonal pyramid (δωδεκαγώνιον πυραμίδα) in a sphere of the colour of night (νυκτόχροιν). This pyramid—every side of which was a regular pentagon—had a door leading into it which was painted with varigated colours (ποικίλαις χρόαις). (See *Philosophumena*, v. 14.) It

pretation thereof: The Mystery which is without in the World, because of which the Universe was made, is all Evolution and all Progress; it projected all emanations and all things therein. Because of it every Mystery exists and the Regions [Lokas] thereof. Come to us, for we are thy fellow members. We are all one with thee. We are one and the same, and thou art one and the same. That is the First Mystery, which was from the beginning in the Ineffable, before it came forth therefrom; and its name is all of us.

" Now, therefore, we all live together for thee at the last Limit; which also is the last Mystery from the Interiors. That also is a part of us. Now, therefore, we have sent thee thy Vesture, which indeed is thine from the beginning, which thou didst place in the last

---

is through this fivefold door that the Soul passes from the Spiritual World, which is now darkness to us because of our ignorance, into the Solar Universe, which was symbolized by the Platonic Solid called the Dodecahedron. This door is of many colours, like Joseph's coat, for what we call colours here below are the witnesses to very real powers or forces in spiritual nature. In the passage from the *Pistis-Sophia* these are referred to as the five " Words " written on the Vesture of the Christos. They are the five attributes of the Spiritual Body of the Yogâchârya School of Buddhism, which will be referred to later on.

Limit, which also is the last Mystery from the Interiors, until its time should be fulfilled according to the command of the First Mystery. Lo! its time being now completed, *I will* give it thee. Come to *us!* For *we* all stand by thee to clothe thee with the First Mystery, and all its Glory by command of the same, because that the First Mystery, coming into manifestation, gave us *two* vestures to clothe thee *besides the one*, which we have sent thee, since thou art worthy of them and art *prior to us, and came into being before us*. For this cause, therefore, the First Mystery sent for thee through us the Mystery of all its Glory, two Vestures."

The text then goes on to detail the Hierarchies and Æons, Powers and Gods, which compose these Heavenly Garments—corresponding detail for detail with the whole emanative potencies of the Universe whereby the Garment of Deity is woven, and then continues its magnificent exposition; the living Powers which form the Vesture speaking as follows on the Great Day " Be with us "—the moment of the Supreme Initiation:

" Behold, therefore, we have sent thee this

Vesture, which no one has known from the First Precept downwards, because the radiance of its Light had been hidden therein, nor did the Spheres and all the Regions downward from the first Precept (know it). Make haste, therefore, clothe thyself with this Vesture. Come to us; for ever, until the time appointed by the Ineffable was fulfilled, we have been in need of thee, to clothe thee with the two Vestures by the Command of the First Mystery. Lo, then, that time is fulfilled. Come, therefore, to us quickly, that we may put them on thee, until thou fulfillest every Ministry of the Perfections of the First Mystery, appointed by the Ineffable. Come to us quickly, we will put them upon thee according to the command of the First Mystery; for the time that yet remains is very short. Thou art coming to us and wilt leave the World. Come, therefore; quickly shalt thou receive all thy Glory, the Glory of the First Mystery."

These three Vestures are the three Buddhic Robes described in the *Voice of the Silence* (pp. 96, 97). They may be described as the Body of Transformation (Nirmâna-kâya), the Body of Bliss (Sambhoga-kâya), and the Body of the

Law (Dharma-kâya). Very little is publicly known of these Transcendent Vestures, even by the Buddhists themselves, so that the accounts we have in the books of various Oriental scholars are contradictory and misleading. The highest is the Vesture of the Law which H. P. Blavatsky tells us is void of all attributes, and describes it as an "ideal breath." If this Vesture is assumed every possible connection with the earth is at an end, and, therefore, the Buddhas of Compassion lay it aside that they may still remain and work on for humanity. Nevertheless, Eitel in his *Sanskrit-Chinese Dictionary* (*sub voc.*, "Pancha Dharma-kâya") speaks of the five attributes of this Vesture—which he calls "the Spiritual Body in five portions" (!)—and describes them as follows:

"1. Precept . . . . exemption from all materiality (Rûpa).

"2. Tranquillity . . . . exemption from all sensations (Vedanâ).

"3. Wisdom . . . . exemption from all consciousness (Sangñâ).

"4. Emancipation (Moksha) . . . . exemption from all moral activity (Karma).

"5. Intelligent views .... exemption from all knowledge (Vignâna)."

In other words, exemption from the five Skandhas or groups of qualities.

These "attributes," it will be seen, are all negations, and the first is, strangely enough, called "Precept," the identical idea preserved in the term "First Precept" used by the Gnostic writer. More, there are five of them, the precise number of "Words" written on the lowest Vesture of the Gnostic narrative.

These three Bodies are the Trinity in every religion. In Buddhism the ineffable Ocean of Light and Compassion is called Bodhi. By bathing or being "baptized" in this, man becomes a Buddha or Enlightened. These three Vestures are thus said to consist of "Essential Bodhi" (Dharmakâya), "Reflected Bodhi" (Sambhogakâya), and "Practical Bodhi" (Nirmânakâya). (See Eitel, *op. cit.*, *sub voc.*, "Trikâya.") And it is the last, the Vesture of Practical Bodhi, which is assumed by the Christs and Buddhas of Compassion who help on man's salvation.

Perhaps it may not be without interest, when remembering the important part played by "sheep" in Christian symbology, to learn that the three symbolical vehicles of the saints across the river of life, or conditioned existence, are said by the Buddhists to be:

1. Sheep, *i.e.*, Shrâvakas — Hearers or Disciples.

2. Deer, *i.e.*, Praty-eka Buddhas—Solitaries, they who obtain salvation for themselves but are unable to impart their wisdom to others.

3. Oxen, *i.e.*, Bodhi-sattvas—they of the essence (Sattva) of Bodhi, or Compassion and Wisdom. (See Eitel, *sub voc.*, "Triyâna." Further information may be obtained from Schlagintweit's *Buddhism in Tibet*, p. 38.)

But the present theme is too lofty a one for a pen like my own, and the Doctrine of the Great Renunciation of the two higher Vestures—to don the comparatively lowly one of the Nirmânakâya—has been treated of, in some measure, in other theosophical writings. What has been said, however, as to these Robes woven of Nature Powers—which are really Human Powers, if we would only "help Nature and work on with her"—what little has been said may perhaps enable us to better understand the grand passage from the *Book* of the Golden Precepts (*Voice of the Silence*, 1st ed., p. 72), which tell us of the birth of a Master, as follows :

.   .   .   .

"Behold, the mellow light that floods the Eastern sky. In songs of praise both heaven and earth unite. And from the four-fold manifested Powers a chant of love ariseth, both from the flaming Fire and flowing Water, and from sweet-smelling Earth and rushing Wind.

"Hark! . . . from the deep unfathomable vortex of that golden light in which the Victor bathes, All Nature's wordless voice in thousand tones ariseth to proclaim :

"'Joy unto ye, O men of Earth. A Pilgrim hath returned back from the other shore. A new Arhan is born.'"—

Feeling himself, his own low self the whole;
When he by sacred sympathy might make
The whole one self. Self, that no alien knows!
Self, far diffused as fancy's wing can travel!
Self, spreading still! oblivious of its own,
Yet all of all possessing.—COLERIDGE.

Out of the furnace of man's life and its black smoke, winged flames arise, flames purified, that soaring onward, 'neath the karmic eye, weave in the end the fabric glorified of the three vestures of the Path.

BOOK OF THE GOLDEN PRECEPTS.

THE WEB OF DESTINY.

How familiar to every child born of Christian parents is the phrase, "God created the world out of nothing"! It is a matter of belief, the reason cannot grasp it; it is absurd and therefore pertains to the domain of faith. *Credo quia absurdum!* And yet I was told by a Jesuit father that it was a "postulate of pure reason"; that as I was a rational being and had heard the truth, it was nothing but the obstinacy of my heart that prevented my acceptance of the dogma, and for that same obduracy I was rightly and properly condemned to Hell. I thought that it was the obduracy and uncharitableness of someone else's heart that so condemned me, and departed less of a "Christian" *of that kind* than ever.

Nevertheless there is good in the dogma, for good and evil are hidden in all things. The good in it is that the human soul shrinks from admitting anything else than God in the boundless fields of being. Nothing but God. And the universe, what of that? "Verily God created it." But how? "Out of nothing—but himself," I think I hear the small voice whisper.

The dogma of "creation out of nothing" has its good side, for it is an attempt, when rightly understood, to bring home to the uninstructed mind the great truth that deity in its own nature does not perform the function of a fabricator, that its "creations" are those of will, transcendent and spiritual, and that the "creatures" of its divine creation in their turn carry out the behests of the divine will, and emanate and evolve, build and fashion, the wondrous fabric of the universe.

The evil side of the doctrine is the use made of it by an ignorant priesthood to dwarf the human mind by ever imposing upon its natural questionings the dull weight of an unintelligible dogma, which crushes its sprouting life and terrifies the half-awakened intelligence with the nightmare of a vengeful deity that punishes every timid turning of the soul to higher light.

Fortunately, however, there has been, long before this curious priest-made dogma (for it is not to be found in the scriptures) was invented, and there still is, another view of the matter which avoids the Scylla and Charybdis of the extremes which I have pointed out above—a view which supplies a golden mean or passageway along which the soul can sail in safety.

In the Vedic scriptures the Eternal is said to have *thought* the universe out of himself, by the self-emanative power of self-contemplation. In other words, the Supreme Being evolved or created the universe out of himself; that is to say, that Deity is both the efficient and material cause of the universe.

Many commentaries have been written upon the Vedas, and the habit of some of them is to argue out the great statements in the original scriptures, bringing forward objection after objection. In fact, in the commentaries, there is a familiar dramatic character who is always turning up, called the "objector." "How then can it be possible," interrupts the objector, "that God can be both the material and efficient cause? The potter makes his pots out of clay. The potter is not the same as the clay; the efficient and material causes are not the same person. The potter does not make the pot out of himself." And then the writer of the commentary replies, using a simile found in the sacred scripture itself, "Even as the spider spins its thread out of itself and withdraws it again, so this universe is spun out of the Supreme and is again withdrawn." It is, however, carefully stated that a simile must not be confounded with an identity. The Supreme does not weave the garment of the universe out of himself in precisely the same manner as the spider spins its web, but the simile of the spider is, at any rate, a nearer approach to the reality than the crude analogy of the potter.

So we read in the *Shvetásvatara Upanishad* (vi. 10): "May the One God, who, like the spider, through his own nature, encases himself with many threads, which are produced by the first [Nature] ; make us one with the Supreme."

And again in the *Mundaka Upanishad* (i. 7): "As the spider casts out and draws in [its web] . . . . so is produced the universe from the Indestructible."

The ideas of a spider and of a web are found over and over again in the sacred books of the Hindus; so much so that it is borne in upon the mind of the careful reader that such a

THE WEB OF DESTINY. 117

frequent simile must correspond to a very important fact in nature. But there is another simile that is even more graphic. It is the figure of the chrysalis and the butterfly, of the silkworm and the cocoon. And here let me quote one passage out of many which will give you a foretaste of what this essay designs to treat of.

The vast Indian epic, called the Mahâbhârata or Great War, is many times larger than the Iliad of the Greeks, and its epic dress is only the setting for long religious and philosophical discourses. One of its great divisions or books is called the Book of Peace, and one of the subdivisions of this Book is entitled the Book of the Laws of Freedom. In it we read as follows:

"As the silkworm spinning its cocoon shuts in itself on every side in every way by means of its self-made threads, even so the soul, though in reality it transcends all attributes, invests itself on every side with attributes [and thus deprives itself of freedom]." (Sec. ccciv.)

This cannot but remind us of the graceful myth of Psyche among the Greeks. Psyche, the soul, painted and sculptured with butterfly wings—the soul that wings its joyful flight from the chrysalis of the body—is a figure so innate with life and beauty that the mind is at once held captive by the sweet graciousness of so fair a conceit.

Let us next turn to another ancient book, fragments of which are given by H. P. Blavatsky, where we shall find the same idea of a web and its spinning. One of the Stanzas of Dzyan runs as follows:

"Father-Mother spin a Web, whose upper end is fastened to Spirit, the Light of the One Darkness, and the lower one to its shadowy end, Matter; and this Web is the Universe, spun out of the Two Substances made in One."

Father-Mother is the graphic name for the Eternal when viewed as emanating the universe out of its own essence. Spirit and Matter are names for the modes of its existence as viewed by little men. Spirit is that Light of which the author of the Book of Genesis speaks as created by the divine fiat that willed "let there be light." It is the Light of the One Darkness, because Spirit is the brightest light that the inner eye of man can bear; and yet beyond this the intuition declares there is that which transcends even this most glorious light, but upon which no mortal can look and live, for to see it he must become immortal. And this is, therefore, darkness to mortal gaze, and so is not inappropriately termed the One Darkness. So, then, Father-Mother spin the web of the universe out of the two substances, Spirit and Matter, which really are not two in essence but one, for they are Father-Mother essentially.

In this connection it is hardly necessary to remind the reader of the words put into the mouth of the Erdgeist by the genius of Goethe:

"Thus at the roaring loom of Time I ply,
   And weave for God the garment thou see'st
      Him by."

This garment of God is the universe. The loom of the Erdgeist roars as the shuttles fly on their cyclic journey back and forth; but their roaring is no chaotic cacophony, but the "harmonious song" of the "spheres."

It may be useful to remark here that with regard to the idea of a cocoon (for the garment or web is ever spheroidal), the symbol of an egg, or embryonic germ, is an index of the same idea, and its frequent occurrence in the old religions is because of the marvellous manner in which so universal a phenomenon in nature shadows forth the manner of the inner workings of the creative energy.

Yet one more instance of the same idea, this time from the hieroglyphics of ancient Khem. Several of the inscriptions on the tombs of the kings in the ancient sacred city of Thebes have been translated by Edouard Naville, the French Egyptologist, and embodied in his book, *La Litanie du Soleil*. A few sentences dealing with the present subject, together with M. Naville's excellent commentary, were translated in the May number of *Lucifer* (1894), under the heading, "The Gods and their Dwellings." Speaking of Teb Temt, the term for the Supreme Being in these old records, M. Naville writes:

"He is a being enclosed in an envelope, which is neither a sphere nor an egg, but more closely resembling the latter. The symbol which represents the envelope Teb has exactly the shape of the cocoon of the silkworm. This is, no doubt, the origin of the tradition handed on to us by Eusebius, which attributes the form of ☉ to the universe."

It would be easy to multiply quotations and

produce much evidence of the frequency of this idea in ancient scriptures, but sufficient has been said to warrant a fuller exposition than if the conception were of very rare occurrence.

Now, the study of the allegorical descriptions of creation and the origin of the universe that are found in every scripture, would be of only minor importance if they had but a remote bearing on human affairs. If primordial processes and the development of long series of hierarchies are simply to serve as a pretext for airy metaphysical speculation, they can only be of interest for a very limited class of minds. If, on the other hand, the processes of the great world are directly applicable to the processes of the little world, if the history of the universe is also the history of man, then the study of such processes is of very vital interest to us, for they teach us the history of the spirit and soul in man, and so wean him from the illusion that he is a mere body, and the powers of man only such as the physical body will permit him to wield. We have all heard the trite old aphorism, commonly called Hermetic, "as above so below," and some have met with it elsewhere and have learned to realise its truth, for it helps the solution of the great problem of life in a manner that no other method will. Analogy of processes and the great fact that man is potentially deity, that "This is That," as the grand logion of the Vedas has it, is the only means whereby a solution of the problem can be attempted; and a religion or a philosophy, or a science, that neglects this central fact ends nowhere but in confusion. As the *Kathopanishad* (II. iv. 10) has it: "What verily is here below that is there; what is there is likewise here." That is to say, what is true of the universe is true of man, what is true of man is true of the universe; what is true of little man, the little world, is true of the heavenly man, the great world.

Let us, then, bear this in mind and apply it to the subject in hand, our "web of destiny." The web of destiny is not one but three, not single but threefold, for are there not three worlds? The threads of the web are gross, subtle, and subtler than subtle, for is not *man* spirit, soul and body? And is not *man* God, did he but know it? There is but one Self "hidden in the heart of all creatures." It is the bodies that make the Self *seem* different, for it *is* one for all. These bodies are webs of destiny, self-evolved, self-woven. There are those who think that man is but his physical body; not so say the scriptures. The seers of truth speak of man as spirit, soul and body, and the wisest say that the Self is beyond. In man, the Self is enwrapped, and yet not really enwrapped—for all words are incapable of truly stating the mystery—in a spiritual body or spirit, in a psychic body or soul, and in a physical body; three webs of destiny, or, if you prefer it, one web of triple texture. The spiritual, psychic and material vestures clothe the Self in a triple disguise that produces this seeming separateness which is called the "great heresy" by those who know the Self. The Vedántic psychologists call them the gross, subtle and causal vestures or disguises, and the early Christian mystics, the so-called Gnostics, classified mankind into the Hylics, Psychics and Pneumatics. These Greek names signified that men were to be distinguished according to the bonds in which they were bound, according to the error in which they were plunged, for Hyle means matter, and Psyche soul, and Pneuma spirit.

But these vestures are living vestures, for there is the material life, and the psychic life, and the spiritual life; three oceans of life and consciousness, and yet not three but one, for they are the Self. For what is more precious to man than life; what does he cling to with such desperation? He clings to the Self, for life is the Self. Through life alone can we have some conception of God here in this world. Life is God.

And so we have three bodies and three lives, the habitual or material life, the emotional or psychic life, and the intuitional or spiritual life, and yet all is one—the Self. Here we have the seven-fold nature of the Esoteric Philosophy, so much talked of and so little understood; and yet it is a natural classification, an unavoidable classification. It is by what the Vedântins call the "false attribution" of the Self to the gross vesture or physical body that the "waking" consciousness, or habitual life, is experienced; by the false attribution of the Self to the subtle vesture, or psychic body, that the "dreaming" consciousness, or emotional life, is sensed; and by the false attribution of the Self to the causal vesture, or spiritual body, that the "deep sleeping" consciousness, or noetic life, is enjoyed. Now these terms "deep sleeping," "dreaming" and "waking" are very inadequate, and are only the reflections or memories of the three great lives, or states of consciousness, in our small brains. For what we call dream is only a memory, and what we call deep sleep is only a reminiscence, a vague feeling, that we have slept ill or well. These three states *appear* to us in our normal consciousness as waking and dreaming and deep sleep; but there is a waking consciousness appropriate to each of the three bodies of man, and a dreaming state, and one of so-called deep sleep; and beyond all is the "fourth," the "peace that passeth all understanding."

Here below in this world we are wrapped round in a triple vesture, for all things centre together here in the battlefield of good and evil. The triple "carapace of selfhood" imprisons and confines us.

In the "interspace," or "middle distance," there are but two vestures, if complete severance from physical bonds can be achieved ; but if not, the shadows cast by the blackness of the sins committed in the body are reflected into the world of the soul and accompany it on its passage through the "hall of learning."

In the highest world there is but one, the vesture of causation; and in this "heaven-world" the disciple learns the past and future. They say the wise ones can separate these three vestures at will, can assume and lay them aside, for the Self strides through the three worlds in the twinkling of an eye.

The mystics of the early days of the Christian era, now condemned as heretics, knew of these sacred things and understood the meaning of the outward rites and symbols. Thus they called those who had no thought for anything but the body and its pleasures the "dead." These were the Hylics, the "sepulchres," for they were indeed dead to higher things; such men and women were naturally without the community of real "Christians;" not placed without by any man-made ordinances, but naturally outside the "church" or assembly of saints. For to enter therein they had to "rise from the dead" and be baptized. This baptism was no outer form; the outer form was but a symbol. It was a real natural process open to all men, not to be given by favouritism, not to be withheld by mortal hands. And there were two great baptisms, the lesser and the greater. The baptism of water and the baptism of fire or of the holy spirit. These were the lesser and the greater mysteries that we hear of among the Egyptians, the Greeks, the Persians and elsewhere. For what is the baptism of water? We know what water is here on earth; but just as the "dreaming" state is but a memory and reflection of the true state of the soul in our waking consciousness, so is the water of the earth a reflection of the true water of nature. "On my soul, gentlemen, ye have never seen the true earth," says Eugenius Philalethes, and he might have added, "On my soul, good friends, ye have never seen the true water of life." For this water is the ocean of soul-life, the "astral" ocean, that causes the soul-sight to live. It was only when the pilgrim had learned to put on his subtle vesture at will and was "doused" into the waters of the ocean of pure astral light and life, that he was indeed baptized with water. And yet these were but the lesser mysteries. Those who were illumined by this *natural* initiation were called Psychics. But the greater mysteries pertained to the perfect, the just. The baptism of fire was the reception of the spiritual influx of divine light and life. The breath of the Holy Spirit (air) vivified and energised their spiritual bodies, and thus they were called Pneumatics.

Beyond these greater mysteries, transcendent and unspeakable as they are said to be, there was something grander and greater and more wondrous. Beyond the three states is the "fourth"; the Self, the Father, is ever waiting on the threshold for his children. It is the mystery of the At-one-ment, the baptism of blood, when the very life and essence of deity is given that man may be one with the Highest. Pity it is that these high things are so degraded in our age. But we are in the mire and must make the best of it.

Let us now return to our three vestures, the karmic webs that we have woven for our weal and woe. The third depends on the second, and the second on the first. The physical body is the product of the psychic, and the psychic of the spiritual. Or in other words, the gross vesture is "precipitated" through the force-mould of the psychic vesture, by means of the character and experience stored up in the spiritual vesture. Each vesture has its appropriate life-span. The "shadow-man" lives longer than the physical, it may be but a few years, it may be centuries, for its life-span is as variable as that of the physical vesture, though its normal life is of greater length. But both these life-cycles are governed by the great life-cycle of the spiritual body. The gross and subtle bodies have their root in the causal. This is the perennial root living throughout the "eternity." On this "all the worlds depend," as the scripture saith, or in other words, from it grow all the bodies, gross and subtle, that serve as vestures for the reincarnating Lord. And seeing that these psychic and physical bodies sprout forth from it and die down into it, as the summer and winter of its great year cause the warm life now to be breathed forth and then to be withdrawn, it needs must be that all causation rests with it; that it is the karmic storehouse of all that each man was, is, and will be; that (to use another simile), it is the very "book of the recording angel." It is because of this that the whole past of a man surrounds him on every side; it is impressed on his psychic vesture (the sidereal or astral man), for it is the "influence of the stars"; it is stamped upon his physical frame and features. But these "stars" are not the stars of heaven, and the predictions of astrologers and cheiromantists and the rest are based on a correspondence and not on a reality. True astrology deals with something higher.

Nor need we go further than the mythology of the Book of Genesis to gain a conviction of the truth of this triple nature of man. For there is first the man made in the "image" of God, and then the Adam of "red-earth," who dwelt in paradise, no physical region as we now understand the word. The paradisiacal body is the soul, and not until man is cast out of Paradise does God lastly fashion for him his "coat of skin." Only when man is born into physical life is he clad in the gross vesture of the material body. Can anyone be so foolish as to think that God actually made for Adam and Eve garments from the skins of animals wherewith to clothe them? Let us leave such crudities to the uninstructed congregations of our "little Bethels," and proceed to see whether it is possible for man to escape from the triple web of his destiny; and how the passivity of the three great oceans of life may be changed into the activity of the three great lights; and how that the triple-tongued flame may burst forth and destroy the webs and join the ineffable Grand Master, the Fire Self.

Perhaps some may think that, as I am writing about destiny, I should therefore, enter into a long disquisition on freewill and necessity; but I have no desire to enter into that endless squirrel-wheel of controversy. Freewill and necessity are mutually dependent; each exists because of the other; remove one and the other ceases to be. They are a pair of opposites, and the best religion and philosophy teach that there is that which transcends all pairs of opposites, and that man in his inmost nature can reach that all-desirable goal which is a solution of the great problem of manifested existence.

But, again, someone may ask, surely this web of destiny is not eternal? By no means; to be eternal, in the absolute sense of the word, it needs must be woven with the shuttle of the eternal will. That is to say, that into all our acts and words and thoughts we must put the whole of the eternal will of the universe.

Surely this is impossible in the very nature of things! That which we think to be ourselves, that which acts in us, is not the Self but that which we think to be ourselves. It is not a reality, but an ever-changing and impermanent something. For no matter how long it may persist, aye, even for an "eternity," it is not eternal in the absolute sense of the word. The Eternal, the One Reality, knows no change.

The web of the universe is woven with the shuttle of divine love—love for all that lives and breathes. It is that deific desire for universal good or harmony; it is a perpetual self-sacrifice, giving of its life and light to all without distinction. Thus it is in the "above," but in the "below," here in the world of men, the shuttle whereby we weave our web of destiny is the shuttle of desire. This is selfishness; a power that concretes, that draws to itself for itself. We weave our webs of destiny from the warp and woof of things of sensation and of matter by means of the shuttle of desire. But as this lower desire is no stronger than ourselves, our lower natures, it cannot be that the fabric it weaves should be eternal. It is made up of ever-changing and impermanent materials, and so must cease when the energy that produced it is exhausted.

What is most important to realise, however, is that this web is a living thing. What we call matter is only negative life; but the web of destiny extends beyond matter into the realms of feeling, emotion, volition and mind. Thought is one of the most important substances from which it is woven. As the *Dhammapada* of the Buddhists says (x. 3):

"All that we are is the result of what we have thought; it is founded on our thoughts, it is made up of our thoughts."

This is the great teaching brought out so powerfully in the Gospel of Christendom; "He who casteth his eyes on a woman to lust after her, has committed adultery already with her *in his heart*." That is to say, in his soul, within in the region of his mind which is so potent a region of his universe. Though this teaching is not explained at length in the Christian canon, in the Buddhist and Vedic canon there are numberless dissertations on the nature and power of thought. One example will suffice. In the *Maitrâyana Upanishad* (vi. 34, Max Müller's Translation), we read:

"Thought alone causes the round of a new birth and a new death; let a man therefore strive to purify his thoughts. What a man thinks, that he is: this is the old secret. If the thoughts of men were so fixed on the Eternal, as they are on the things of this world, who would not be freed from bondage?"

This is the same teaching as that of the Sermon on the Mount: "The pure in heart shall see God."

This vesture of thought and the rest, then, is a very real thing. It is alive, it lives in us. This was also the belief of ancient Egypt. After the death of the body, the soul was said to pass forth on its path through the different regions of the Amenti. Just as the soul had shed off its body, so did the spirit shed off its psychic vestures, as it passed back into its own state, and these vestures, just as the body here below consists of countless "lives," consisted of living "beings," were woven out of living threads. In the *Litany of the Sun* already referred to, mention is made of "prayers to divers *beings* which have to serve as envelope to the essence of the Defunct."

And now the question arises, "If this is so,

how is it possible to avoid for ever weaving this awful web of destiny more and more densely round ourselves. Thoughts come into our mind unbidden. It is impossible for one to get rid of them."

Now in the Roman Catholic Church there is a teaching that there is no sin, if a man does not join his "will" to the thought. This is precisely the teaching of the other religions I have referred to, and is consonant with the whole of what I have previously written. There is a continual procession of thoughts ever passing through our minds—empty shapes, shadows and images. We can reject these shadows and let them pass on or arrest them by fixing our attention upon them. If we go further and give our consent to them we put our desire into them, and so breathe into them the breath of our life. They then become part of us, we have ensouled them, they are our children. If our desire is selfish and impure, then these children of ours are of a like nature, and we weave round ourselves and into our nature evil and impure forces.

I know that these things have been written of over and over again, but the story will not spoil for retelling. As we live, every moment we give birth to that which will be our self in a future existence and a future life. We give birth to a child. And if we, the dual parent of this child, are impure, passionate and immoral, the child we generate will be of like nature. Just as diseased and immoral parents, parents who procreate children in drunkenness and in obedience to the dictates of mere animal lust, give birth to abortions, crippled, lunatic and vicious children, so does each one of us give birth to an abortion if we are slaves of our desires. But if, on the other hand, we strive to transmute our lower desire into the divine love and will, then we may give birth to a divine child which will in time grow into the full stature of the Heavenly Man. This is the "second birth," the spiritual creation, spoken of by the Christ in the Gospel. This is why the Brâhmans, not those who are born into a physical caste, but those who truly know Brahman, or the Eternal, are rightly called the "twice-born."

Yes, we can escape from our web of destiny by weaving for ourselves the glorious vesture of the spirit, the "wedding garment," the "coat woven without seam of the Christ."

As the Book of Peace (*Mahábhárata*, Shânti Parvan, Mokshadharma Parvan, cccci.) says:

"By casting off, through the aid of Yoga, these five faults—attachment, heedlessness, covetousness, lust and wrath, a man attains to freedom. As large fishes, breaking through the net, pass into their own element [to sport in blessedness], after the same manner Yogins [breaking through the net of lust, wrath and the rest] become cleansed of all sins and attain to the blessed state of freedom. As powerful animals, breaking through the nets with which the hunters surround them, escape into the blessed state of freedom, after the same manner Yogins, freed from all bonds, attain to the sinless path that leads to liberation. Feeble beings, entangled in acts, are surely destroyed. Even such is the case with those destitute of Yoga-power. As weak fishes, fallen into the net, become entangled in it, even so men destitute of the power of Yoga, encounter destruction [amid the bonds of the world]. Bound by the bonds of their acts, they that are weak meet with destruction, while they that are possessed of strength break through them."

"The kingdom of heaven is to be attained by violence." Yoga means union, the striving for union with the divinity that is in the heart of all creatures. This is the at-one-ment that is the consummation of all religion. Yoga-power is the strength of the spiritual life, the energizing of the divine will. It is to be developed by "brooding" upon it; by service of the Eternal, that is, by dedicating the whole of one's life to the Self; and by faith, that is, by faith and confidence in the possibility of such union.

It is said that the Supreme Being created the universe by means of such brooding (Tapas). By wrapping oneself round with this great spiritual power, by ever living in it, by realising the great Presence of the Eternal, the germ of the divine child will develop within. This brooding is the formation of a virgin womb, from which the immaculate child shall be born. This brooding is also heat and fire. It is thus that the three streams of life and consciousness (see p. 124) no longer continue as passive oceans of external existence, each on its own plane, but change into active energies which become three fires, or rather a triple-tongued flame that finally blazes forth into the great fire and light of the universe.

Without doubt we can cast off our old garments of desire and stand in the purified robes of divine will and universal compassion. To cast off our old squalid raiment we must practise non-attachment to it. We must be willing to stand naked before our Self, and this we cannot do unless we love that Self. There is a negative and a positive method to be followed. The practice of non-attachment to the things of matter, to our possessions in this world, and to all that we think is *ours* within, is absolutely necessary, but this alone is not sufficient, it must also be accompanied by the positive love of the highest and the best, of the Self within. Both these forces are necessary. But there is danger even here, there is danger that a man should seek that Self for himself alone, should love that Self that so he may gain salvation for his own sake. Therefore it is, that he who would gain true wisdom, and live and realise the Self here on earth, must learn to love that Self in all that lives and breathes and not in himself alone. Then and not till then will he be on the path of final liberation from the delusion of that spiritual ignorance which causes him to weave his web of destiny.

This is the doctrine of the Christ, the saviour, the spirit within, the one from whom the many come if we could but understand it. This is also the teaching of Egypt of old. To quote yet once more from the inscriptions on the tombs of the kings of ancient Thebes:

"The kingly 'Osiris' is an intelligent essence; those who are born from him create him; they rest when they have caused the kingly 'Osiris' to be born."

The kingly Osiris is that highest vesture of the Self, the spirit or spiritual body. It is the causal vesture, the karmic record, from which the soul proceeds. The personalities all come forth from the divine individuality according to that karmic record. The many came forth for the one. This is the perennial root from which we came forth and into which we return, and by "we" I mean the "I am I," the person we *think* we are for one life, and not the real "I am" that is for the eternity. This "I am" is an "intelligent essence." "Those who are born from him" are our personalities, and it is the personal man who, by his efforts at self-purification and aspiration to this divine prototype within, shall grow like unto the spiritual man. So that at last he shall become at one with the Christ within, and so "create" the kingly .Osiris. And then shall we be at "rest," then shall we have found refuge in the "Self of Peace," then shall we have reached that "peace of God that passeth all understanding," and the web of our destiny shall be the same as that of the self-made and self-appointed destiny of God.

Deum te igitur scito esse.
Know then that thou art God.
     Cicero, Somnium Scipionis.
Om! Peace, peace, peace!

TRUE SELF-RELIANCE

A STUDY FROM CICERO AND THE UPANISHADS.

What am I? Whence came I? Whither do I journey? Verily, the voice of one crying in the wilderness, mourning, and not to be comforted either by the lifeless dogmas of an effete theology or the cold denials of a materialistic science. It is from the sages of old, from the wise of the past, that the answer comes. That art thou. From That didst thou come. Into That shalt thou return. Aye, That art thou! That is thy Self, none other. Such were the final words whispered into the ear of the disciple in the golden days of ancient Âryâvarta. True then, true countless ages before, true for the rest of the eternity. Nowhere else is to be found true Self-reliance, nowhere else that peace which none can take away.

A cold creed! do I hear some one say? Nay, not cold. It is a truth that transcends enthusiasm, that surpasses all hope, that merges the highest ideal of love into an endless, boundless compassion for all that lives and breathes. For thus runs the Upanishad:

"Now will I tell thee the ancient mystery of the Highest. . . .

"That true Man, who wakes when we sleep, accomplishing every desire—that is called the Shining, the Highest, the Deathless. In that all the spheres are contained, and no one goes beyond. Aye, this [true Man] is That [the Universal Soul].

"As fire, though one, on entering into the world, [pervading] form after form, takes the form [of what it enters], so the Inner Self of all creatures, though one, takes on shape after shape, and yet [remains] apart.

"As air, though one, on entering into the world, [pervading] form after form, takes the form [of what it enters], so the Inner Self of all creatures, though one, takes on shape after shape, and yet [remains] apart.

"As the sun, the means by which the whole world sees, is not sullied by the outer impurities which our eyes behold, so the Inner Self of all creatures, being one, is not sullied by the misery of the world, but [remains] apart [from it].

"It is this Inner Self of all creatures, the Lord of the Will, who, though one, causes the one form to appear manifold. The wise who find this abiding in themselves, theirs is blessedness everlasting, and not others'.

"The eternal among the non-eternal, the conscious among the unconscious, who, though one, fulfils the desires of many. The wise who find this abiding in themselves, theirs is peace everlasting, and not others'.

"'This is That'—so runs the burthen of their thoughts—the transcendent bliss that beggars all description." (*Kathopanishad*, Adhyâya ii., Vallî v. 6-14.)

The Upanishad then proceeds to explain that this Higher Self is self-luminous, and the cause, not only of the light on earth, but also of that in the heaven. The Self shines *by its own light*, it is *self-motive* within.

This is the secret of true Self-reliance; nowhere else is a lasting basis to be found, nowhere else unchanging certitude. In this self-motivity resides the essence of immortality and nowhere else; it is the one spark of divinity in man. A man must grow from within without, for such is the law. All other growth is artificial and unnatural, deceptive and illusory.

No one from without can give us peace and blessedness; these must perforce come from within, from the Inner Self of all creatures—our true Higher Self.

Even should a Master—a Jīvanmukta, one who has attained union, while still in the body, with that Higher Self—cast the mantle of his power round the disciple, should he wrap him in his aura, even then, it were to no profit, if the disciple is not ready to burst the veils of his Soul with *self-effort*.

If the nature of the disciple does not respond of its own will, and grow of its own energy, the artificial exaltation would be not only unprofitable but even injurious. For the instant the protecting wall were removed, the reaction would sweep the unprepared neophyte off his feet. The passions and desires that had been curbed and held back by the external power of the teacher would fiercely spring forth, and the lassitude of the pupil's will, following the artificial stimulus, would be unable to check their wild career. And that is why it is so difficult even for a Master to interfere with the natural growth of the disciple. This is what is meant by saying that even sages *dare* not interfere with the growth of karmic seeds. Nature must work on in her own way, and growth must proceed *from within without* and never from without within.

This applies to all of us, especially in the mental attitude we take up in Theosophy. The perfect fruit of nature is the birth of the true Man. It is no artificial creation, but a natural steady growth; a birth with pain and sorrow, with mighty throes suffered and joyfully endured. But to be perfect it must be *self-born*, it must be divine, and that which is born from another than the Self is other than divine, subject to death and decay.

We *must* work out our own salvation, wisely, humbly, nobly. There are no swaddling clothes for the Self, no apron-strings to tie the soul to; from the very beginning it must walk of itself, of its own energy and force. There is no spoon-meat, no nursing, no whimperings to be hushed. It is a *Man*, no animal embryo. It strides forth as a giant from the egg that envelops it.

They who have conquered are Shepherds of Compassion, not sheep, are Lions of Mercy, not deer. They are the Christs and the Buddhas, and it is their will that all shall be like unto them, all be one with them.

Let us not, then, weakly repeat the words of others, and reflect the thoughts of others, but if the words are good and the thoughts wise, strive to develop in ourselves the spirit that dictated such words or induced such thoughts. The Lodge does not wish for the mere monkey-dom of external imitation, or the parrot-like repetition of words. It requires companions on whom reliance can be placed, because such companions rely on that Self which is the Self of the Lodge.

The secret of the Self is that it is self-motive. As Cicero writes, repeating the noble doctrine of the Stoics and of the Mysteries:

" Strive on, with the assurance that it is not thou who art subject to death, but thy body. For that which is really thyself is not the being which thy bodily shape declares. But the real man is the thinking principle of each, and not the form which can be pointed to with the finger. Of this, then, be sure, that thou art

God; inasmuch as deity is that which has will, sense, memory, foresight; and rules, regulates and moves the body it has in charge, just as the Supreme Deity does the Universe. And like as Eternal Deity guides the universe, which is in a certain degree subject to decay, so the sempiternal soul moves the destructible body. Now that which is ever in motion is eternal. Whereas that which communicates motion to something else, and which is set in motion by an external cause, must necessarily cease to exist when its motion is exhausted."

And then (as Macrobius says), repeating the *Phædrus* of Plato, word by word, Tully continues:

"That, therefore, which has the principle of motion in itself, seeing that it can never fail itself, is the only eternal existence, and, moreover, is the source and causative principle of motion to all other bodies endowed with movement. The causative principle, however, can have no antecedent cause. For all things spring from this principle, which cannot, in the nature of things, be generated from anything else: for if it were so, it would cease to be the principal cause. And if this is without beginning, it can evidently have no end, for if the principle of causation were destroyed, it could not be re-born from anything else, nor give birth to anything out of itself, for all things must necessarily be generated from the causative principle. The principle of motion, therefore, comes from that which is endowed with self-movement; and this can suffer neither birth nor death; otherwise every heaven would collapse, and every nature necessarily come to a standstill, seeing that it could no longer obtain that force by which it was originally impelled.

"Since, therefore, it is evident that that only is eternal which is self-motive, who is there to deny that this is a rational attribute of souls? For everything that is set in motion by external impulse is destitute of the soul principle, whereas everything ensouled is energized by an interior and self-created motion; for this is the soul's proper nature and power. And if it alone of all things has the attribute of self-movement, it surely is not subject to birth but is eternal."[1]

---

[1] From *The Dream of Scipio*, in Cicero's *De Republica*, vi. In commenting on this passage, Macrobius (*Commentarius in Somnium Scipionis*, II. xiii) gives a number of syllogisms which may be useful to set down here.

But there are those who rely on their intellect, on their strength, on their wealth, or position, their beauty, their relatives or their friends. This is not true Self-reliance, for all these pass away.

Intellect will fade in its turn, just as the body fades in its small cycle, for:

"Thou art the sheath of the Highest, [which in its turn is] enveloped in the intellect." (*Taittiriyakopanishad*, Vallî i, Anuvâka i. 1.)

Intellect is but an envelope, a veil to be removed, a garment to be purified, before the true Self shines forth.

Strength and wealth and position and beauty are even more impermanent: strength and beauty fade even before the body wears out, and

---

1. The soul is self-motive: Whatever is self-motive is ever in motion: Therefore the soul is ever in motion.
2. The soul is ever in motion: Whatever is ever in motion is immortal: Therefore the soul is immortal.
3. The soul is self-motive: Whatever is self-motive is the principle of motion: Therefore the soul is the principle of motion.
4. The soul is the principle of motion: Whatever is the principle of motion is not subject to birth: Therefore the soul is not subject to birth.
5. The soul is not subject to birth: Whatever is not subject to birth is immortal: Therefore the soul is immortal.
6. The soul is self-motive: Whatever is self-motive is the principle of motion: Whatever is the principle of motion is not subject to birth: Whatever is not subject to birth is immortal: Therefore the soul is immortal. (Aurelii Macrobii *Quæ Extant Omnia*, Patavii, 1736.)

wealth and position must be abandoned when Yama speaks the word.

Friends and relations, parents, husband, wife and children, are but weaklings like ourselves—to mourn and rejoice with—all subject to the sway of Death. There is but one place of peace, but one source of true reliance.

"That place [of peace] which all the sacred writings sing of, proclaimed by all who strive to purify their nature, for the sake of which men enter the service of the Highest, that place [of peace] will I in brief recount to thee. It is the 'Om.'

"Aye, that word is the Highest, that the Supreme. He who knows this, all that he longs for is his.

"That is the best on which to rely, that the most excellent. He who relies on that, waxes great in the heaven-world.

"He, the [harmonious] singer, is not born, he dies not. He [came] not any whence, nor any one was he. Unborn, eternal, everlasting, ancient—this is not slain when the body is slain.

"If the slayer thinks he slays, or if the slain thinks he is slain, both are deluded. *He* slays not, nor is slain.

"Smaller than small, greater than great, is

the Self of a man, hidden in the secret chamber [of his heart].

"It is by the favour of the Lord [the Logos] that a man beholds the majesty of the Self, [but only when he is] without preconceived notions and free from distress.

"Sitting It goes far, resting It journeys everywhere. Who but myself can know that which rejoices and rejoices not.

"The wise man who regards the Self as bodiless among bodies, as ever-abiding among the fleeting, as the mighty Sovereign, he grieves not.

"This Self is not to be obtained by much instruction, nor by intellectual study, nor by holy writ. Him whom It enfolds by him is It gained. The Self enfolds the very soul of the man.

"But he who has not turned his back on evil-doing, who is not at peace, and not controlled, who is not of quiet mind, he, even with knowledge, cannot gain It." (*Kathopanishad*, Adhyâya i, Vallî ii. 15-24.)

It is in the Self that we find the source of all moral sanction. It is the "still small voice" —"the voice of the silence"—the voice that grows into a roar of thunder if the Law is transgressed. Then it becomes the "great terror"—the one thing that the disciple fears, for it is by the Law of his higher nature that he *condemns himself*—to continued bondage in the meshes of the karmic net he has supplied threads for the weaving of by neglect of duty. As in the Great World so in the little world, as in the Universal Self so in the individual self, as in the Kosmos so in man. "That art thou!" As It emanated Itself, so dost thou emanate thyself, O little man! Thou canst give birth to Chaos or to the Son of Righteousness, and thou wilt. Therefore, choose. Transgression of the Law creates difference, and so a departure from the Self; union with the Law provides the conditions for the Self to show forth its glory. Learn, then, from what takes place in the Great World "unconsciously," what must be done in the little world by the *conscious will* of him who would be free.

"In the beginning this [manifested world] was non-existent. Thence, verily, the existent arose. That made its own self. Wherefore is it called the self-made. Now that self-made verily is essence, for only when a man attains to the essence is he filled with blessedness. For who could live, who could breathe, if that

TRUE SELF-RELIANCE.

blessedness were not in the quintessence [of the heart] ? For it is that which causes blessedness.

"For when a man finds fearless reliance in that which no eye can see, which transcends all selves, which cannot be defined and which needs no support—then has he ceased from fear. Whereas, should a man make were it but a speck[1] within It—then fear arises for him. This is ever a terror for him who knows and ponders upon it.

"For thus says the scripture: 'From terror of That the wind blows, from terror the sun rises.'" (*Taittirîyakopanishad*, Vallî i, Anuvâka viii. 1.)

And again:

"The whole emanated universe trembles in Its Breath, That is the Great Terror, an up-raised thunderbolt. They who know it, become immortal." (*Kathopanishad*, Adhyâya, ii, Vallî vi. 2.)

For no man can flee from the Self, no man can escape from his conscience. The Law enfolds him in his own doings, from which there is no escape until he takes refuge with that Law. As the King-Psalmist says:

[1] This expression is given up by the commentators and translators. I would suggest that it may mean the most simple organism, which modern science affirms to be little else than a sac or "stomach." The trained seers and initiates of old were familiar with such primary organisms *psychically*.

"Whither shall I go from thy spirit? or whither shall I flee from thy presence?

"If I ascend up into heaven, thou art there: if I make my bed in hell, behold, thou art there also." (*Psalms*, cxxxix. 7, 8.)

For:

"That which is down here in a man and that which is over there in the sun, both are one.

"He who thus knows, on leaving this sphere, first passes into the food-self, thence into the life-self, thence into the sense-self, thence into the mind-self, thence into the self of blessedness, and identifying himself with the spheres beyond, experiencing what he wills,[1] assuming whatsoever form he desires, he sings this hymn:

"'Hâvu, hâvu, hâvu! Food am I, food am I, food am I! I am the food-eater, the food-eater, the food-eater! I blend them, I blend them, I blend them![2] I am the First-born of Righteousness. Before the gods was I in the centre of the Immortal. He who gives me, verily he preserves me. I consume him as food, who consumes food.

---

[1] Lit., "eating whatever food he desires."
[2] That is to say, I am object (food) and subject (food-eater), and I am the union of both object and subject, the one consciousness.

TRUE SELF-RELIANCE.

"'I have flooded the world, I the Golden Light. So even does he who thus knows.'" (*Taittiríyakopanishad*, Valli iii, Anuvâka x. 4-6.)

He who has thus conquered, who has become the First-born of Righteousness, who verily is a Twice-born (Dvija), a true Knower of the Highest (Brahma-vid), he verily is:

"The [true] Sun in the Highest—[for] thus stands the doctrine, and thus the exposition thereof.

"In the beginning this was non-existent. The non-existent then became existent. It developed. It turned into an Egg. It lay for the measure of a cycle. It broke in twain. The halves were one of silver, the other of gold...

"Thence was born the Sun. When he was born shouts of joy arose." (*Chhândogyopanishad*, Prapâthaka iii, Khanda i. 1-3.)

Here we have the whole story of the spiritual evolution in man. The darkness of the soul before it begins to long for final release, for true wisdom. The alchemical separation of the subtle from the fixed, of the higher from the lower, of Spirit from Matter, and the birth of the unclouded Mind, the Son of Righteousness. Only when the Master is born do all the Powers rejoice and a mighty shout of gladness rends the universe. Aye:

"In Him, heaven, earth and the interspace are woven, and the sensory with all the life-currents. Know Him alone as the Self; away with other words. He is the Bridge to Immortality.

"There [in the heart] where the currents (Nâdis) meet, like spokes in a nave, He moves about within, becoming manifold. Chanting the 'Om,' thus meditate on Him. May all blessing attend you to cross beyond the darkness!

"He the all-wise, the all-knowing, to whom is all the glory in the world, He is the Self, established in the shining city of the Highest, in the quintessence [in the heart].

"He is ensheathed within the sensory, is ruler of the envelope of the life-currents, and finally rests in [the outer sheath of] nutriment. It is by meditating on the heart, that the wise by their knowledge behold that Blessed Immortal Form which shines forth [to their sight].

"The knot in the heart is loosed, all doubts are solved, and all deeds (Karma) perish, when a man once sees the vision of that which is both high and low.

"In the highest golden envelope dwells the

passionless, partless one, the Highest. He is the pure Light of all lights, and that they know who know the Self.

"In that [Light] no sun shines, nor the moon and the stars, nor shine those flashings over there, much less this earthly fire. It is because of the shining of this Self that all shines after it, by its shining that all this is so bright.

"This, the immortal Highest, is before, the Highest is behind, to the right hand and to the left, gone forth above and below. The Highest is verily all this. It is the best!" (*Mundakopanishad*, Mundaka, ii, Khanda ii, 5-11.)

The doctrine is mystic and mysterious, the antipodes of the *apparent* clearness of modern scientific theories, "for the gods love mystery and hate familiarity," as Rishi Yâjnavalkya says in the *Brihadâranyaka*. And yet again more mysteriously than ever:

"There, in the quintessence, within the heart, dwells the [true] Man (Purusha), of the nature of mind, immortal, resplendent like gold.

"There, above the palate, like a breast-nipple it hangs—that is the Womb of Indra.[1]

---

[1] The "astral fire."

160 THE WORLD-MYSTERY.

"There, where the ends of the hair start, having passed through the skull, chanting 'Bhûh,' he is supported in Fire ; chanting 'Bhuvah,' in Water ; chanting 'Sûvah,' in the Sun ; chanting 'Mahah,' in the Highest.

"He obtains kingship over himself, he obtains lordship over the mind. He becomes lord of speech, of sight, of hearing, of understanding.

"Thence he becomes that Highest whose body is quintessence, the true Self, that sports in life, of blissful mind, immortal, in perfect peace." (*Taittiríyakopanishad*, Valli i, Anuvâka vi, 1, 2.)

And yet once again, to finally remind us of the nature of true Self-reliance, reliance on the Self—that Self which :

" Does not age with the age of the body, nor is it killed with the wounding of the body. That is the true city of the Highest. In it all desires are contained. It is the Self, sinless, ageless, deathless, griefless, hungerless and thirstless, willing the True, desiring the True." (*Chhânvogyopanishad*, Prapâthaka viii, Khanda i, 5.)

www.ingramcontent.com/pod-product-compliance
Lightning Source LLC
Chambersburg PA
CBHW031455160426
43195CB00010BB/990